Why Mugabe Won

The 2013 general elections in Zimbabwe were widely expected to mark a shift in the nation's political system and a greater role for the opposition Movement for Democratic Change (MDC), led by Prime Minister Morgan Tsvangirai. However, the results surprisingly came overwhelmingly in favour of long-time President Robert Mugabe, who swept the presidential, parliamentary and senatorial polls under relatively credible and peaceful conditions. In this book, a valuable and accessible read for both students and scholars working in African politics, and those with a general interest in the politics of the region, Stephen Chan and Julia Gallagher explore the domestic and international context of these landmark elections. Drawing on extensive research among political elites, grass-roots activists and ordinary voters, Chan and Gallagher examine the key personalities, dramatic events and broader social and political context of Mugabe's success, and what this means as Zimbabwe moves towards a future without Mugabe.

STEPHEN CHAN OBE was the Foundation Dean of Law and Social Sciences at SOAS University of London, and was 2010 International Studies Association Eminent Scholar in Global Development. He was 2015 Konrad Adenauer Chair of Academic Excellence at Bir Zeit University and 2016 George Soros Chair of Public Policy at the Central European University. A former member of the Commonwealth Secretariat, he helped invent modern electoral observation at the independence elections of Zimbabwe in 1980, and has published 31 books, several on Zimbabwe.

JULIA GALLAGHER teaches African Politics at Royal Holloway, University of London. Her research focuses on African international relations and their impact on domestic politics, as well as British policy in Africa. She is the author of four books on Africa and Zimbabwe, including *Zimbabwe's International Relations*, a forthcoming publication, also with Cambridge University Press.

Why Mugabe Won

The 2013 Elections in Zimbabwe and Their Aftermath

STEPHEN CHAN
SOAS, University of London

JULIA GALLAGHER
Royal Holloway, University of London

CAMBRIDGE
UNIVERSITY PRESS

CAMBRIDGE
UNIVERSITY PRESS

University Printing House, Cambridge CB2 8BS, United Kingdom

One Liberty Plaza, 20th Floor, New York, NY 10006, USA

477 Williamstown Road, Port Melbourne, VIC 3207, Australia

314-321, 3rd Floor, Plot 3, Splendor Forum, Jasola District Centre, New Delhi - 110025, India

79 Anson Road, #06-04/06, Singapore 079906

Cambridge University Press is part of the University of Cambridge.

It furthers the University's mission by disseminating knowledge in the pursuit of education, learning and research at the highest international levels of excellence.

www.cambridge.org
Information on this title: www.cambridge.org/9781107539808
DOI: 10.1017/9781316338025

First published 2017
First paperback edition 2020

A catalogue record for this publication is available from the British Library

Library of Congress Cataloging in Publication data
Names: Chan, Stephen, 1949- author | Gallagher, Julia (Lecturer in international relations), author.
Title: Why Mugabe won : the 2013 elections in Zimbabwe and their aftermath / Stephen Chan, SOAS, University of London; Julia Gallagher, Royal Holloway, University of London.
Description: Oxford : Cambridge University Press, 2017.
Identifiers: LCCN 2016059632 | ISBN 9781107117167 (hardback)
Subjects: LCSH: Presidents–Zimbabwe–Election–2013. | Elections–Zimbabwe–History. | Mugabe, Robert Gabriel, 1924- | ZANU-PF (Organization : Zimbabwe) | Tsvangirai, Morgan, 1952- | Movement for Democratic Change (Zimbabwe) | Zimbabwe–Politics and government–1980-
Classification: LCC JQ2929.A5 C489 2017 | DDC 324.96891/051–dc23 LC record available at https://lccn.loc.gov/2016059632

ISBN 978-1-107-11716-7 Hardback
ISBN 978-1-107-53980-8 Paperback

Contents

Preface

As this book goes to press, President Robert Mugabe seems to be nearing the end of his long rule in Zimbabwe. At 93 his health is poor, and he is beginning to lose a grip on the party he has dominated for more than 40 years, and the country he has ruled for more than 35. Yet only three years ago, Mugabe was celebrating a historic victory in presidential and parliamentary elections that saw him re-assert his dominance over the country after years of fractious inter-party competition, and four years of a precarious and bad-tempered coalition with the rival Movement for Democratic Change (MDC). The MDC's leader Morgan Tsvangirai, once viewed as a heroic and viable alternative to Mugabe, was humiliated in those elections. His political demise was immediately evident in their aftermath. Mugabe, then triumphant, would have a few more years to wait until his own end became inevitable.

The 2013 elections were remarkable on many counts. They represent a substantial shift in Zimbabwe's fraught electoral history, which has been characterised by violence and malpractice since at least 2000. They were unexpectedly peaceful, even good-humoured; although there was evidence of malpractice and some rigging. It is also clear – as we argue in this book – that the outcome was by and large a reflection of the will of the Zimbabwean people. The heavy wins for both Mugabe as presidential candidate, and his party Zimbabwe African National Union – Patriotic Front (ZANU-PF) in parliamentary and senatorial elections, were a dramatic departure from the dismal showing for both in 2008. Between 2008 and 2013, therefore, there was a dramatic swing in popular attitudes towards the parties and their leaders.

It seemed important to us that we try to understand what led to these changes – and this is what the book sets out to do. But more than this, 2013 marks an important point in Zimbabwe's history, possibly the last election for Robert Mugabe, who helped bring the country into being and has, more than any other one person, shaped its identity and history. And so the book also situates 2013 within the political history of the country and its region. It explores the broader social, political and international trends that both explain the outcome of an extraordinary set of elections, and will continue to be shaped by it for years to come.

There has been extensive analysis of Zimbabwean elections since the country's birth. Kriger (2005), Makumbe (2006) and Ndlovu-Gatsheni (2012) each trace the decline in electoral probity since 1980, turning the country's elections into what Ndlovu-Gatsheni terms 'empty rituals' (1). Their work builds on a plethora of excellent studies of individual elections, including Sylvester (1986) on 1985, Sachikonye (1990) on 1990, Makumbe and Compagnon (2000) on 1995, Waldahl (2004) and Rich Dorman (2005) on 2000 and 2002, Kriger (2008) and Berting (2010) on 2005, and Chigudu (2012) and Masunungure (2009) on 2008, 'the most controversial and violent' elections in the country's history (Masunungure, 2009: 1).

Mugabe won all but one of these elections (the 2000 referendum on constitutional change). He did it because of his ability to appeal to the electorate, but was also able to use his power to abuse and subvert the electoral process where necessary. Zimbabwe's elections have been as controversial and surprising as they have been regular.

In 2013, the elections were extensively prepared for and widely speculated on in a way not seen since the early 2000s. Opinion polls, including those conducted by foreigners, suggested that, in a clean contest, ZANU-PF could win. The debate within ZANU-PF was not about the full-scale rigging seen in 2008, but how little rigging could guarantee an outcome that looked possible but not fully certain. Certainly, both South Africa and other regional leaders had issued stern warnings that 2008 could not be repeated. Some in ZANU-PF were tempted all the same to 'muscle' a path to victory, but the decision seems to have gone in favour of judicious rigging. Judicious rigging, but scaled back from 2008, meant the party had to be attractive as well as manipulative; it had to put policies before the electorate – and much work went into crafting and selling them.

The MDC, in turn, was convinced that the rigging of 2008 would be reprised, albeit with less violence. The MDC strategy was not to seek to counter dishonesty, but to complain vociferously to the international community that rigging was underway and that a ZANU-PF 'win' could only be regarded as a stolen result. For Morgan Tsvangirai's forces, there was less emphasis on internal policies to be put before the electorate; they focused energy on how the election should be interpreted for and by external actors.

This book is about how the 2013 elections were won fairly and unfairly by ZANU-PF; and how they were lost ineptly by the MDC against a backdrop of social and political change across the country and region. The authors visited Zimbabwe seven times in 2013 and were there for all stages of the election itself. They draw here upon their expertise, experience and contacts, as well as electoral observation methodologies that reached back to the inaugural election of 1980, and their years of living either in Zimbabwe or in neighbouring Zambia. What follows is their joint verdict.

Acronyms

AU	African Union
CIO	Central Intelligence Organisation
CSO	Civil Society Organisation
EU	European Union
GNU	Government of National Unity
ICG	International Crisis Group
IMF	International Monetary Fund
MDC	Movement for Democratic Change
MDC-N	Movement for Democratic Change – Ncube
MDC-T	Movement for Democratic Change – Tsvangirai
NGO	Non-Governmental Organisation
SABC	South African Broadcasting Corporation
SADC	Southern African Development Community
ZANU	Zimbabwe African National Union
ZANU-PF	Zimbabwe African National Union – Patriotic Front
ZAPU	Zimbabwe African People's Union
ZCTU	Zimbabwe Congress of Trade Unions
ZEC	Zimbabwe Electoral Commission
ZESN	Zimbabwe Election Support Network
ZUM	Zimbabwe Unity Movement

I Introduction
Thinking a New Zimbabwe

> Elections are evil, they cause deaths, they create joblessness,
> homelessness, property is destroyed, the civil liberties of people are
> eroded, the rule of law is suspended. I can't imagine having an election
> again. It's a dreaded experience.[1]

This comment is a reflection on Zimbabwe's 2008 elections, the most
violent and contested in its history. It was made by a man who works
with some of the poorest communities in Harare, many of which had
borne the brunt of state-led violence, and had suffered great hardship
under the economic meltdown that accompanied it. When he made it,
in 2011, members of these communities had just about managed to
achieve a measure of stability. The idea of more elections, planned for
2013, was unimaginable.

Yet those elections did take place, and they were remarkable,
and remarkably different from those in 2008. For one thing, the 2013
elections were not marked by overt violence and disruption; they were
reasonably good-tempered and even marked by moments of humour.
What's more, although there were accusations of rigging – and evidence to suggest substantial irregularities – they have been broadly
accepted internationally as delivering an outcome that reflected the
will of the Zimbabwean people. Most remarkable of all, they delivered
an overwhelming victory for Robert Mugabe and his ZANU-PF party,
and a crushing defeat for Morgan Tsvangirai and the MDC, the man
and party that many argue had really won the 2008 elections.

This book explains how this happened. In telling the story of the
2013 elections, we tell the story of how Zimbabwean politics shifted
so dramatically in five short years. For many reasons, these are

---

[1] Civil society activist in an interview in Harare, 30 August 2011 (JG).

important elections to look at, both for what they tell us about the politics of Zimbabwe and for the broader themes that emerge about modern politics in the region. For Tsvangirai and the opposition, 2013 was supposed to be the 'break-through moment', the final push that would see them overturn a tired and discredited ruling party, in power for more than 30 years. For Mugabe, entering his eighth election in his 90th year, the moment represented a last stand, the moment of judgement on a political life. For many in his party, and their colleagues in the security sector, defeat would mean an end to power and possibly the personal security and material wealth it brought. This election was therefore of enormous personal and emotional importance to both party leaders; for the political elites more generally, the material and security stakes were high.

It was politically highly significant too, coming after five years of a power-sharing government, an arrangement patched together by the region's leaders after the violence and rigging of the 2008 poll. The Government of National Unity (GNU) had been an uncomfortable alliance, marking out a period that often felt like a time of waiting – transition, many people called it – for the moment of decision. Which way would the country go – back to the patriotic nationalism of ZANU-PF that had seemed so discredited in 2008, or towards the Western-style social democracy of the MDC?

The election was also a test of the region's ability to manage and sanction an electoral process. This election was more than usually marshalled by the leaders of the southern African countries (SADC),[2] led by South Africa's president Jacob Zuma. They had been instrumental in clearing up the mess created after 2008; they had watched over a constitutional reform process, and they had tried to ensure that the 2013 process would take place in an orderly, fair and democratic fashion. Their ability to do these things was a test of how far they could manage their own problem cases, to turn Zimbabwe into a more

---

[2] SADC is the Southern African Development Community and comprises Angola, Botswana, the Democratic Republic of Congo, Lesotho, Madagascar, Malawi, Mauritius, Mozambique, Namibia, Seychelles, South Africa, Swaziland, Tanzania, Zambia and Zimbabwe.

peaceful and stable regional actor and to provide ballast for the region's democratic credentials more generally.

Finally, the elections were a moment for the West to re-evaluate its relationship with Zimbabwe. After the bitter rows with Mugabe's government since the 1990s, and the sanctions and pariah status meted out to it as a result, 2013 was potentially the moment of re-engagement, re-investment: the resumption of normal relations. This was something that most Western donors wanted to see; the European Union (EU) demonstrated its eagerness by quietly relaxing sanctions in the run-up to the poll. An MDC government would allow an immediate return of Zimbabwe to international donor favour; any president other than Mugabe would at least open up interesting potential for friendlier relations.

In the end the result was a stunning validation of Mugabe and ZANU-PF, an expression of distaste for compromise government, and a crushing rejection of Tsvangirai's modernisation programme. Mugabe gained enormous political credibility from the result – he was quickly elected president of SADC and then of the African Union (AU), and was able to control a succession battle that emerged in his party two years later. Tsvangirai was flattened by the result, helplessly standing by as his party 'hit the delete button'. It is now difficult to see the revival or emergence of any Zimbabwean opposition in the medium-term.

Internationally, the election provided a solid success for the region and beyond it – delivering a twenty-first century African election that was widely judged to have been reasonably peaceful and credible. And it left Western donors with a conundrum: to accept Mugabe's mandate and re-engage, or not? It is possible to imagine that ZANU-PF's election victory has provided a key moment in the assertion of African control over its own affairs.

THE THEMES THAT GUIDED THE ELECTIONS

The book deals with several important themes that formed the backdrop to the 2013 elections. Loosely, these can be grouped into conditions, characters and relationships.

The key conditions that shaped the 2013 elections begin with the legacies of colonialism. Despite the fact that Zimbabwe has been independent since 1980, the country's politics continue to be dominated by structures and relationships inherited from the colonial era. The fact that the ruling party and its leaders were forged through a violent anti-colonial war still shapes the rationales of government – its tendencies to fall back on the security apparatus, its hierarchical rigidity, and the continuing importance of the war credentials of its key members (Bratton, 2014). More widely, the ruling party's anti-colonial identity finds resonances among Zimbabweans, particularly in rural areas where the war was most keenly experienced. Mugabe himself is still highly valued as the war leader who led his people to independence. This independence legacy is closely linked to land redistribution, which began in 2000 when groups of war veterans marched onto white farms and evicted their occupants. This was the moment that Mahmood Mamdani (2008) has controversially described as the point of Zimbabwe's 'true independence', as if by expelling the white farmers, the country could return to an authentic, pre-colonial identity.

The anti-colonial rhetoric has been part of Mugabe's repertoire since the late 1990s when he engaged in a standoff with the British government and then parts of the Commonwealth, the EU and other Western donors.[3] As a political tool it bought him domestic and regional support, although many Zimbabweans take it with a large pinch of salt. As one Harare resident put it: 'He doesn't believe that, but they just want to brainwash people, to put something into people's mind so they can remain in power. He's just power-hungry I think. Long back, they used to believe him but not now. He's been promising this and that, but there is nothing.'[4]

---

[3] Few international relationships have involved name-calling on such a scale as that between Robert Mugabe and Tony Blair's governments. The point at which Mugabe was calling Blair a 'toilet' and likening Britain to a sea monster, while members of Blair's government were calling Mugabe's regime 'uncivilised' and a 'basketcase', what Tendi calls discourses of 'demonisation' (Tendi, 2014), must mark a low point in the history of diplomatic exchange.

[4] Mbare resident, Harare, 2 September 2011 (JG).

However, the message was employed with some success in 2013 in government attacks on 'neo-colonial' sanctions employed by the West. Many Zimbabweans remain ambivalent about this, but it is a live debate, and one that played an important role in 2013.

Alongside this legacy are more recent memories of the economic disaster that reached its peak in 2008 with runaway inflation, financial collapse and severe food shortages. Part of the disaster is put down to unscheduled compensation payments made to war veterans in 1997, and part to the collapse in agricultural exports that followed the land seizures from 2000. Some Zimbabweans blame the World Bank and IMF Economic Structural Adjustment Programme introduced in 1991, some the drought of the same year, while others think it was the president's wife Grace Mugabe who ruined the country with her lavish shopping trips to London – a signifier of the extravagant consumption patterns of the ruling elites in recent years. The government tends to blame Western sanctions. But this mixture of economic mismanagement, sour international relations and bad luck led to what the majority of Zimbabweans describe as a nightmarish time when businesses collapsed, salaries became worthless on the journey from the bank to the shops, or in the time it took to queue to buy food, and people lived on *maputi* (popcorn) and soya beans. These traumatic events left many Zimbabweans feeling profoundly insecure.

The Zimbabwe dollar was abolished shortly after the 2008 elections, and the US dollar and South African rand formally adopted. The economy has stabilised, but memories of the meltdown condition Zimbabweans' fears about their still shaky hold on economic viability. Even in 2011 after the economy had found a precarious stability, people still felt rocked by what they had been through. During conversations carried out in the course of research for this book, people reflected on the social and psychological damage that had been done: 'Everything is just muddled'; 'Everywhere we walk around there are problems everywhere as if this is not the country of our birth'; 'It's like death everywhere'.[5] Rumours about plans to reintroduce the Zimbabwe dollar, or about the return of Western investment can cause waves of anxiety or excitement.

The year of 2008 also saw the era of Zimbabwe's worst electoral violence, and this is the third background condition that informed attitudes in 2013. Sachikonye (2011) has provided a careful and painful account of Zimbabwe's history of violence, exploring its origins in the liberation war in the 1970s. These were manifest early on through the factional disagreements between ZANU and ZAPU – the two branches of the anti-colonial struggle – and led to a vicious government clampdown on a largely fictional insurgency in the ZAPU stronghold of Matabeleland in the mid-1980s. Operation Gukurahundi, undertaken by the country's feared Fifth Brigade, led to the death or disappearance of 20,000 people and fixed an ethnic animosity that remains potent today. Violence also played a key part in the invasions of white farms in 2000, and in the razing of poor urban areas in Operation Murambatsvina in 2005, seen by many as an attempt by the government to disperse and demoralise opposition support. Violence became part of the electoral contest, helping mould the polarised party politics between the MDC and ZANU-PF from 2000 (LeBas, 2011). Beatings and arrests of opposition politicians and activists became almost normal at this time – many will remember the striking pictures of the MDC leader Morgan Tsvangirai emerging from police custody in 2007 to speak to the press, dishevelled and battered, with a bloodied and bruised face. In the elections of 2008, after Tsvangirai won more votes than Mugabe in the president poll, forcing the president into a run-off, the security forces and ZANU-PF militia unleashed a brutal wave of violent retribution against parts of the country that had voted for Tsvangirai, leading to his withdrawal from the contest and leaving the presidency to Mugabe by default. Memories of a period that has traumatised many Zimbabweans remained near the surface in 2013.

---

[5] Civil society activist, Harare, 30 August 2011; Highfields resident, Harare, 1 September 2011; Chitungwiza resident, 4 September 2011 (JG).

The second theme we explore, and which plays a critical part in understanding the 2013 elections, is that of the characters of the main actors. These range from the government elites through civil society activists down to ordinary voters.

Mugabe himself continued to be a toweringly important figure in Zimbabwe. Not only did he exercise masterly control over his own party, and over political events in the country, he had huge importance in the region (evidenced in his election as president of the SADC in 2014 and of the AU in 2015), and continued to dominate and to a large extent manipulate Western policy towards his country. Mugabe is a controversial character who has often been misunderstood in the West. His brutal political methods and his management over economic chaos are only part of the story: Mugabe inspires respect among many of his own people, as well as throughout Africa for being a highly intelligent and politically brilliant politician who is unusually ready and able to stand up to the West. Zimbabweans can express deep disgust and hatred for him – one women asked us in 2011, 'Can they not do what they did to Saddam Hussein? I would like to see Mugabe hiding in a hole in the ground'.[6] But even his fiercest critics express admiration for him on occasion, as did this man in a discussion just before the 2013 election about Mugabe's possible defeat: 'It will be sad to see him go. That is a great man. He could have been greater than Mandela – if he had known when to leave office.'[7] Mugabe's dominance, despite the fact that he was nearing his 90th birthday, is a key part of the story of the 2013 elections.

The second key political figure was MDC leader and former trade unionist, Morgan Tsvangirai. He has been the most successful opposition leader in Zimbabwe's history, building a viable party within a handful of years, and beating Mugabe in the first round of the presidential election in 2008. He is respected for his personal courage, and his refusal to make the death of his wife in a suspicious

---

[6] Chitungwiza resident, 4 September 2011 (JG).
[7] Harare resident, 19 July 2013 (JG).

car accident into political capital.[8] But Tsvangirai has personal and political flaws. His party split in 2006 over arguments about his leadership style. And after entering the coalition GNU in 2009, he was often described as indecisive and easily manipulated by Mugabe and his colleagues. Stories about his colourful love life after the death of his wife added to the impression that his mind was not fully on his job as prime minister, and the growing comfort and corruption among his MDC colleagues in government caused anger among his supporters, many of whom felt betrayed by their leaders.

A wider cast of characters also played crucial parts in this story: Solomon and Joice Mujuru, the powerful husband-and-wife team at the heart of ZANU-PF, who came under suspicion for being too reformist; Emerson Mnangagwa, their rival for the succession, and the man many Zimbabweans fear would make an even more brutal president than Mugabe; and Tendai Biti, the technocratic MDC Minister of Finance, who many credit with stabilising the Zimbabwean economy, but who became locked with Tsvangirai in a fierce battle over the direction of the MDC. Others led a range of breakaway opposition forces, such as Welshman Ncube, the leader of the rival MDC faction, and Simba Makoni, one-time ZANU-PF loyalist, who stood as an independent candidate for the presidency in 2013. Finally, in the months leading to the elections, the sudden Facebook appearance of a figure named Baba Jukwa provided a mischievous twist to the elections. His political gossip appeared grounded enough to suggest he was a renegade 'insider' of the highest ZANU-PF circles. On the eve of polling, he advised his followers and Facebook friends to vote MDC. He may well have been the creation of the circle around Vice President Joice Mujuru, setting the stage for an eventual post-election struggle with Emerson Mnangagwa for the succession to Mugabe. Personalities – material and virtual – are the lifeblood of any election.

---

[8] Many believe the accident was a botched assassination attempt on Tsvangirai himself.

Election analysis often concentrates on political elites, but elections are unusually a time where the opinions and activities of the population come to the fore. So a further crucial 'figure' discussed is that of the Zimbabwean people. A lot of the discussion in this book is based on interviews with grass-roots activists, civil society leaders and ordinary voters. Many have been badly treated by government policy and repression in recent years; many too have benefitted, for example, from land reform which gave small-scale farmers access to livelihoods unknown for generations. Zimbabweans are politically savvy. Some of them are weary of politics and deal with elections by keeping a low profile until it is all blown over. Some engage enthusiastically in the process, seeing opportunities for political expression and material advancement unavailable at other times. Others, despite brutal treatment and bitter experiences of defeat and stolen elections, remain engaged and optimistic about the power of elections to change their lives. We explore what Zimbabweans made of the policies and personalities on offer, and we discuss their analysis of why the election turned out the way it did.

The final theme explored in this book is that of relationships. Here we have a complex web of relationships – within the coalition government itself of course, with the dynamics of power-sharing a new challenge for ZANU-PF, and a particularly difficult one for the inexperienced MDC. The ways in which Mugabe first sidelined, and then tamed Tsvangirai form another important backdrop to 2013.[9] At the same time, the relationships between the parties and their political followers were gradually but radically altered over the years of coalition. ZANU-PF's steady and persistent efforts to reconnect with voters, and to mobilise supporters, reportedly began as early as 2008; the MDC's neglect of its core voters, and its gradual but devastating

---

[9] There are several good accounts of the transition period in Zimbabwe. For example, see Murithi and Mawadza, 2011; Masunungure and Shumba, 2012; Raftopoulos, 2013; Chan and Primorak, 2013.

dissociation from the concerns of ordinary Zimbabweans, also had dramatic consequences for the outcome in 2013.

Crucial too were relationships within the SADC region. The GNU had been organised and imposed by SADC under the leadership of South Africa's Thabo Mbeki. The region's leaders continued to play a role in shaping the fortunes of the GNU, and were to provide a vital alibi for the elections themselves: the verdicts of SADC and AU observers on the quality of the democratic process were of great importance to Zimbabwe's regional status, which would reflect to the wider world as well as back into the country itself. SADC leaders, and their relationships with Zimbabwe's key political players, were of more than usual importance in 2013.

Other international relationships played a role too. Although they were less powerful in determining domestic relationships, the Western countries' decisions over whether and when to ease sanctions were pored over, used and misused by Zimbabwe's political leaders. Sanctions, although targeted at ZANU-PF figures, were an effective tool in Mugabe's narrative of Western imperialism. They were used to distinguish between ZANU-PF's patriotic nationalism and the MDC's equivocations over land reform and relationships with Western supporters. This message finally began to gain traction, so that although it had once been an asset for the MDC, in 2013 Western support was more of a liability.

The final relationship discussed here is that between state and society. This is about how Zimbabweans feel about themselves, both as subjects of an authoritarian political regime and as masters of their own fate. Here is a story of ambivalence: one of hopefulness and world weariness; fear and loathing, and love and respect; nostalgia and attachment to patriotic history and a desire to move the country on; idealisation of the West and an acknowledgement of fit within the region; respect for or fear of violence and desperation for a more ordered state–society relationship; a need and desire for material wealth along with an idea of a Zimbabwean moral status; the feeling of regional superiority and the fear of becoming the regional joke.

Given their history, the hardships they have faced in recent years, and their political sophistication, the story of Zimbabwean identity is a complex and compelling one. Most telling of all is the fact that, for many Zimbabweans, Mugabe himself still embodies all of these contradictions. He has shaped the country, and he continues to define it. This fact is key to understanding the outcome of the 2013 Zimbabwean elections.

This is an account of an election, but it is also the portrait of a country and its impact on a region. In looking at it as we do – through the moves, manipulations, successes and failures of the parties' leaders, and through the views and decisions of ordinary Zimbabweans – we have drawn a detailed picture of the country. In particular, this picture examines the nature of leadership in Zimbabwe. It tells the story of how Mugabe has managed to dominate the country into his 90s, and how the more youthful and charismatic Tsvangirai failed to convince people that he could lead it. This despite disastrous economic collapse and political violence under Mugabe's watch, and the widespread support for Tsvangirai that almost saw him win the presidency in 2008. Why, in the final showdown between the two, did Mugabe win so convincingly?

A CONCEPTUAL FRAMING

Some scholars explain ZANU-PF's victories in terms of structuralist accounts of power – those proposed by David Moore (2006) and Brian Raftopoulos (2013), for example, which focus on the material attributes of power. These emphasise Mugabe's control of the security forces and the patronage networks that tie people into the ruling party as deciding factors in his electoral success. Without denying the importance of these factors, our account also draws on more culturalist understandings, the most sophisticated of which explore the ways in which power is produced through imagination. Here we borrow from Schatzberg's understanding of 'moral matrices ... against which people come to understand the political legitimacy, or "think ability", of institutions, ideas, policies, and procedures' (2001: 1).

Schatzberg argues that political cultures across 'middle Africa' view political authority as similar to paternal authority.[10] He traces popular and elite discourses about the president-father of the nation-family; the father's job is to feed and nurture his 'children', but also to discipline them when necessary. His legitimacy rests on his ability to do this. If the population is fed and cared for, the president is an object of respect, 'it becomes increasingly unthinkable to challenge them' but

> when they violate the implied cultural norms and unarticulated expectations of political 'fatherhood', their legitimacy erodes; tensions mount; and instability, repression, or both ensue. Under these circumstances, it becomes all too thinkable to contemplate the removal of a political figure who has violated the trust and expectations implicit in the moral matrix of legitimate governance. (2001: 203)

Such a situation clearly pertained in Zimbabwe during the 2005 and 2008 elections, and many people described the country as a dysfunctional family. As one respondent put it: 'The president is like a father, but this one has kicked all his children out.'[11] In particular, the young are leaving: 'People don't think there is any solution for them yet, in the medium-term. In this region most people are no longer staying in this country. The young people want to go out – they have surrendered.'[12] The political failures translated into family failure: many people couldn't feed their families without help. One trade union organiser who hadn't received her salary for more than two years said: 'I've got a sister in the Netherlands and two daughters in Cape Town: that's how I keep going ... I'm like a useless mother to my own

---

[10] Schatzberg's account of political legitimacy covers eight countries stretching across tropical Africa from Senegal in the west to Kenya in the east. He suggests that his argument holds across this part of 'middle Africa', without wanting to extrapolate to the whole of sub-Saharan Africa. However, much of his argument has strong resonances with Zimbabwe.

[11] Chitungwiza resident, 28 August 2011 (JG).

[12] Religious leaders, Bulawayo, 29 May 2012 (JG).

children.'[13] Zimbabwe, for much of the 2000s, has felt like a dysfunctional family whose father refused to provide, indeed, one who had
'kicked his children out', with a 'useless mother' who was unable to
provide, and children who had 'surrendered', given up and left. In such
a situation, it did become 'thinkable' to evict Mugabe from office. His
inability to provide had lost him legitimacy; he could no longer claim
to be father of the nation.

However, just five years later everything looked different. The
economy had stabilised and the violence had subsided; the situation
wasn't nearly as desperate. And then ZANU-PF unleashed a charm
offensive on the country. Its leaders travelled up and down, reconnect-
ing, apologising and promising reform. They brought gifts and they
crafted policies that would ensure material well-being. Their ability to
provide, and to project the capacity to provide, was (as we detail in
Chapter 5) a key part of their successful appeal to the electorate. This
reconnection is often described in emotional terms – conveying the
rediscovery of a proper sense of self, it became possible to become
'Zimbabwean' again. The fact that Zimbabweans remained perfectly
aware of the violent underside of ZANU-PF's authority did not detract
from this sense. Schatzberg would understand it in terms of the
disciplining role of the president-father, a feature that does not neces-
sarily undermine his legitimacy, as long as he is still able to provide
for his children. Mbembe has depicted postcolonial politics across
much of the continent in similar terms, focusing on the ambiguity
of political authority. States, he suggests, are viewed both as providers
of protection and moral superiority, 'organizer[s] of public happiness'
(2001: 31), and wielders of arbitrary violence, woven into the allocation of privileges. His suggestion of this as a complex relationship and
a complex basis for the imaginary of the state resonates with current
conceptions of state–society relations in Zimbabwe.

However, it would be too easy to slip into an account that
described the choice Zimbabweans faced in 2013 as being between an

---

[13] Trade union organiser, Bulawayo, 28 May 2012 (JG).

African-style account of power and legitimacy epitomised by Mugabe as the 'father-president', and a Western, legal-bureaucratic account of power represented by Tsvangirai. This might have seemed a more reasonable division of politics in the mid-2000s, when the polarisation created between the two parties had appeared to offer a stark choice to the voters (LeBas, 2011). But most Zimbabweans have a more complex understanding of political authority, drawing on an attachment both to the legal order represented by their state institutions, and an acceptance of patronage networks rooted in familial, ethnic and regional ties: the 'economy of affection', in Hyden's terms (2006). This ambivalence has been addressed by McGregor (2013), who discusses the complex mixture of patrimonial and rational-bureaucratic paradigms negotiated by Zimbabwe's civil servants. Likewise, Primorac and Chan (2013) describe Zimbabwean politics as 'hybrid', a process and set of ideas that need to be understood as a tension between a desire to throw away the past and a desire to maintain its preeminent place in the public imagination. The impossibility of choosing between 'two sides' was a feature of 2013: Zimbabweans expressed an ambivalent approach to the state, one which reflected both the desire that it should 'feed' them and that it should be ruled within a rational-legal framework.

The picture is further complicated by the considerable fear that underwrites political relationships in Zimbabwe. Although these elections were peaceful, fear was a hidden subtext, particularly in poor urban areas, and in ZANU-PF's rural heartlands. Fear can be a part of how the state–society relationship is conceived, as Schatzberg suggests, or it can be a constraint on the ability of ordinary people to express themselves politically. In 2013, it was both.

Tsvangirai, it was clear from his time as prime minister, had ceased to be a thinkable president in 2013. His love affairs, his apparent lack of concern at the growing corruption of MDC representatives in national and local government, his inability to instil discipline on his party – none of this represented him as a good father figure, or president. The criticism of Tsvangirai and the MDC (which we detail in Chapter 4) focuses on the lack of capacity – the party didn't have the resources to look after the electorate – and weak leadership, as well as the sense of alienation engendered by what were seen as 'foreign' political priorities and campaigning methods.

This is not to say that Mugabe suddenly came to embody an unambiguously ideal president in 2013. It is important not to push the polarisation argument too far. Mugabe might have looked like the antithesis to Tsvangirai in 2008, but many Zimbabweans continue to have a far more complex understanding of the man who has led them for so long. Mugabe represents both a nurturing/repressive father-figure *and* the best embodiment of Westernised sophistication. His manners, command of the English language, intelligence and ability to conduct himself on the world stage are a source of pride for many Zimbabweans. 'Mugabe is more English than the English.'[14]

This is why so many people voted for Mugabe, a man who has presided over economic ruin, political violence and misery for millions of people. And it is why they rejected a man who is widely acknowledged to be personally courageous, and who, in joining the GNU, helped stabilise a nightmarish political and economic situation, bringing some measure of order. In the end, when Zimbabweans looked at the two men running, they couldn't see Tsvangirai as president of Zimbabwe – it wasn't 'thinkable'. He didn't have the educational credentials, political sophistication, historical embeddedness or regional standing of Mugabe. He didn't encapsulate their idea of Zimbabwe. Mugabe, with all his complexity – his cold savagery, his brilliant rhetoric, his projection of power, and his ability to embody a new, independent, confident country – did.

A NOTE ON METHODOLOGY

Both authors of this book have been following Zimbabwe's politics for many years – Stephen Chan (SC) was involved as a young Commonwealth diplomat at the Lancaster House talks in 1979, and Julia Gallagher (JG) went there as a graduate to teach in a rural secondary

---

[14] Chitungwiza resident, 28 August 2011 (JG).

school in 1990. Both have continued to visit the country ever since, and have written widely on its politics.

To this book we mainly bring research carried out from 2011 – the middle of the GNU period – up to 2015, two years after the election. We both visited the country at least annually over this period, with more intensive research undertaken in 2013 itself. We have divided the labour between us according to our contacts and expertise. Chan engaged mainly in elite interviews with senior political figures and those watching from diplomatic, media and academic circles, based largely in Harare. Gallagher explored grass-roots attitudes, drawing on her networks of political and civil society activists around the country.

Harare is a gossip mill, where information and misinformation are often difficult to disentangle, and where rumour and fact are interchangeable. Chan's research is gathered through off-the-record briefings and informal meetings. His networks enable him to read the undercurrents of newspaper reports and to negotiate between what is fact, what is likely and what is improbable. Much of his contribution to the book is told in a broad-brush narrative style in order to preserve the anonymity of his sources who would be easily recognisable if quoted. Much of the interpretation of media sources contained in Chapter 9 and in the Postscript should be read with this in mind.

Gallagher's research follows a more conventional approach of interviews and focus groups. Interviews were carried out with political and civil society activists, and with ordinary voters in the two largest cities, Harare and Bulawayo, in the dormitory cities of Chitungwiza and Old Pumula, and the rural areas of Matabeleland South and Mashonaland Central.[15] Interviews were semi-structured,

---

[15] These locations were chosen in order to capture differences in attitude between both urban/rural and Shona/Ndebele voters. Harare and Bulawayo have been MDC strongholds in the past, but Harare lost several key constituencies to ZANU-PF in 2013. Mashonaland in the north of the country has consistently voted for ZANU-PF and Matabeleland in the west voted overwhelmingly for the MDC parties in 2008, but saw a dramatic shift towards ZANU-PF in 2013.

and conducted in a mixture of one-to-one and group encounters. Most of the research for this aspect of the book was carried out through interviews in the run-up to the election, three months after it, and one year on. In some situations, people were anxious about expressing political views in front of colleagues, and opened up more fully in a one-to-one situation. However, many interesting accounts came from group interviews with political activists where members of the group found themselves dissecting the elections properly for the first time, and in which discussion often became animated and even heated. Interviewees were invited to tell the story of the elections, and left to define the key elements for themselves. This provided a subjective account of the elections, and we do not attempt in our analysis to explore the validity of what was said. The real names of individuals and organisations have not been given.

Because of the different research methods used, much of the book is structured like a conversation between elites and the wider population. Readers will be able to trace which author is leading on each chapter, because we each represent a side of this relationship. The chapters where Chan leads reflect the opaque nature of elite, capital-based politics, while the chapters where Gallagher leads privilege the often-neglected voices of ordinary voters and grass-roots activists.

Putting these various sources together, we have been able to construct an account of 2013 that reflects a broad range of Zimbabwean opinion. Our research combines a discussion of the facts of the election – we draw on sources such as newspapers, academic and think-tank reports, polls and public records to describe these where necessary – and an exploration of how the election looked and felt to the people involved. For us, Zimbabwe's 2013 election is largely constructed through the views and ideas of the people involved. We believe this is an appropriate way to understand an election, a event in the life of a country in which the stories told – by politicians and voters about themselves, each other, their country and their international partners and enemies – are at least as constitutive of the election as any material factors. Although you will find statistics on things like turnouts, vote share and campaign budgets, and accounts of political rallies and Facebook campaigns, 2013 can only be fully understood through the stories.

Chapters 2 and 3 reflect on the build-up to the elections and the elections themselves. Most of the analysis in these chapters builds on Chan's interviews with senior Zimbabwean politicians and foreign diplomats posted to Zimbabwe. We trace the volatile years that led up to the 2008 elections, and discuss the working of the GNU – the uneasy alliance between the MDC parties and ZANU-PF – that followed them, before moving on to an evaluation of the 2013 elections themselves, as seen from Harare. Chapters 4 and 5 move away from Harare to explore the outcome from grass-roots perspectives, from urban, peri-urban and rural areas. These chapters, based primarily on Gallagher's fieldwork in November 2013, begin to piece together the reasons for the MDC's catastrophic losses, and to explain why many voters turned to ZANU-PF – many for the first time. Chapters 6 and 7 change tack again, providing an overview of the academic and think-tank analysis of the 2013 elections, exploring questions about rigging, party strategies and voter attitudes. Chapter 8 provides a retrospective on the elections from the grass roots one year on. This chapter draws largely on Gallagher's fieldwork in July 2014, and considers the longer-term effects of the elections on voters' feelings about their government and state. Chapter 9, the final chapter, based again on Chan's research, returns the discussion to Harare. It considers the succession battles that began to take shape within both the main parties in 2014, and considers the prospects of democratic politics in Zimbabwe as Robert Mugabe inevitably nears the end of his life.

2   Building towards the 2013 Elections

The 'harmonised' elections (presidential and parliamentary together) of 2008 saw the opposition party of Morgan Tsvangirai, the MDC, approach its ninth birthday and what now looks like the last peak of its electoral popularity. It had achieved early success in the constitutional referendum of 2000, which it won; it then fought and lost the parliamentary elections of 2000, the 2002 presidential elections and the 2005 parliamentary elections. Despite successive losses, the MDC had become a powerful and persistent presence in Zimbabwean politics.[1]

The rigging in the 2005 elections was considerably more complex than in 2002. The presidential race involved two main candidates, but the 2005 parliamentary race involved 120 seats in a 150-seat chamber (30 being appointed by the president). In 2005 the

---

[1] At the first independence elections in 1980, Robert Mugabe's ZANU won a resounding victory over the predominantly western, Ndebele-speaking party, ZAPU. Succeeding elections were for many years accepted by the West as free and fair. This was despite atrocious military pogroms from 1982 to 1987 to crush supposed armed dissidence in the Ndebele region; and despite much local thuggery in the 1990 elections, when Mugabe was challenged by an old comrade, Edgar Tekere, and his new but short-lived ZUM party. Domestic support remained strong too: the 1990 elections would have been won by Mugabe and ZANU-PF with or without thuggery. It is fair to say that there was no need for nation-wide election rigging throughout the first 20 years of independence; there was no opposition party sufficiently challenging to necessitate it. In 2000, however, with the growing popularity of a new opposition party, Mugabe was finally defeated at the polls for a first and only time. The new MDC, led by Morgan Tsvangirai, won a referendum on constitutional reform called by Mugabe. It became almost a confidence vote in the President. Zimbabwe's politics would never be the same. In every subsequent election, rigging and violence have played sufficient roles for the outcome to be decisively swung in Mugabe and ZANU-PF's favour. Violence and rigging reached an apogee in 2008, when the MDC was bludgeoned with extreme force and the counting was distorted so significantly that Morgan Tsvangirai was clearly prevented from becoming Zimbabwe's rightful president.

MDC claimed it should have won 62 seats, but the official results gave the party 41. Even if the MDC had gained all 62 seats, and thus claimed electoral victory over ZANU-PF and its 57 seats (there was one independent seat), Mugabe could still appoint 30 more MPs, giving ZANU-PF 87 MPs and a house majority of 24. With only 41 seats, however, the MDC could not muster a 'blocking third' in parliament, and ZANU-PF could thus move constitutional changes through the house. It seemed the objectives of rigging did not include reducing the MDC to nothing – there was still much to be gained in presentational terms of having a 'democratic' system with a 'viable' opposition – but to prevent it from having sufficient force to oppose ZANU-PF on the most important constitutional issues.

Rigging came of sophisticated age in 2005, but MDC mistakes were also beginning to assume a pattern. These mistakes bear some discussion. The party, built on the back of the trade union movement, had an urban base and never really broke out into rural areas; it never developed policies that spoke to the conditions of rural life. Even in its urban base, not all of its seats were secure; the imposition of unpopular candidates could see 'safe' seats lost to ZANU-PF – such as Harare South. Total vote share could have been higher for the MDC, but it never conducted any significant voter registration drives, and many people in urban electorates were turned away at the polling stations for not having been registered. The MDC support in the Ndebele-speaking west of Zimbabwe was an anti-Mugabe vote, but the MDC did not develop specific policies for the western provinces and, despite attracting the majority of the votes, the MDC could not increase voter turnout beyond about 50 per cent and, by and large, voter turnout for the 2005 elections was, in the western provinces, slightly down on 2002.

Maintaining support, and then maximising support, should have been two MDC priorities – while, for ZANU-PF, electoral strategy would have included containing and then constraining MDC support in key urban areas, keeping on top of voter registration, and in control of the rural areas, and in dividing the MDC support in the west. However, the ZANU-PF government, despite its electoral strengths and command of electoral strategy, could not make government work in the parliamentary term that began in 2005.

MELTDOWN IN ZIMBABWE

The 2005 elections were held in March. In May, Mugabe's ZANU-PF government displayed a curiously tragic version of its middle-class and upper-middle-class aspirations and sensibilities by launching Operation Murambatsvina.[2] This razed the ghetto suburbs of the country's main cities, mainly MDC strongholds at that point, but did so on the public rationale that the thriving informal sectors they were home to had erected many buildings without planning permission and had created a series of urban eyesores. This rationale was widely promulgated and became a frequent recourse in conversation:

> It was ugly, and it was unplanned, illegal in fact – because planning permission had never been granted. And why should respectable and law-abiding people have to look at a slum on their way to work, especially when it shouldn't be there?[3]

This kind of discourse is not confined to Zimbabwe. A similar remark was made to one of the authors (SC) in Lusaka, Zambia, while driving through a slum settlement.

> But you see, this shouldn't be here. It should go away. The government or the municipality should give them funds to build elsewhere, or at least to build something better. It shouldn't be so close to a main route. Decent people don't need to see this.[4]

The difference was that, in Zambia, the government did not send in bulldozers to clear the slums, whereas in Zimbabwe it did. And the

---

[2] There is a broad and thoughtful literature on the causes and effects of Murambatsvina. See Bracking (2005), Potts (2006), Kamete (2009) and Rich Dorman (2016). The UN special envoy, Anna Kajumulo Tibaijuka, produced a critical report on the effects of Operation Murambatsvina.

[3] Senior Zimbabwean business figure, Johannesburg, 10 June 2012 (SC).

[4] Zambian banking executive, Lusaka, 17 June 2012 (SC).

Zambian interlocuteur did include the proviso that accommodation should be provided elsewhere, whereas in Zimbabwe several thousand people were left homeless.

Quite apart from a debate as to whether Operation Murambatsvina was to reduce the MDC vote in its strongholds, the questions we wish to tackle centre on how a ruling party that carried out such a brutal act could so quickly regain its credibility. How could it break the link between such an attack on MDC strongholds and the large numbers of MDC-supporting members of the middle class, particularly in light of the economic meltdown that accompanied it? Why did middle-class voters then begin to desert the MDC? In particular, what was there about the ZANU-PF programme as the years passed that gradually made it attractive to the urban aspirational classes? How were middle-class sensitivities and sensibilities captured? How, by the time of the 2008 elections, with hyperinflation estimated in January 2009 by the *Financial Times* as 6.5 quindecillion novemdecillion per cent could there be any foundation for a middle-class affiliation to ZANU-PF just five years later? How could there be a middle class at all under such circumstances? And why, as we shall see, during the 2008–13 term, when an MDC Minister of Finance stabilised the economy, did this accomplishment not attract more of the middle-class vote? These are questions which raise their head as decisive in the 2013 elections, and we shall come to that. Before then, as 2005 broached into 2006, the MDC was preoccupied with fighting and diminishing itself.

In 2006, the MDC split. The breakaway faction was led by Welshman Ncube, a brilliant professor of law. At first, the reasons were grounded in Ncube's dissatisfaction with Tsvangirai's decision-making processes. These were, Ncube said, not transparent and, in terms of the MDC founding documents, unconstitutional. In fact, Tsvangirai had long deployed a parallel decision-making process, a 'kitchen cabinet' of his own choice that could make decisions faster than the elected party executive (Raftopoulos, 2007). But the track record of this kitchen cabinet was not impressive and left the leadership open to criticism from many of the party faithful. The second tier of Ncube's objections to the MDC was that it lacked technocratic vision. Tsvangirai had been a trade union leader without high formal education, and his style of opposition was to be robustly reactive to ZANU-PF. Ncube wanted a modernising vision, and that accorded with the decision of his new faction to appoint Arthur Mutambara as its leader – recalling the former student leader from the diaspora, where he had made a huge reputation as an Oxford graduate (he had gained an Oxford doctorate), an American professor of robotics and a South African businessman. Quite apart from the technocracy embodied in the choice of Mutambara, he was also untainted by political scandal and corruption. He had no 'baggage'. Ncube was canny enough to know that he, as an Ndebele leader, could not attract sufficient of the eastern Shona vote for his new faction to break through in the 2008 elections, but he hoped Mutambara could. While many criticised Ncube's lack of loyalty, few voices disagreed with his analysis of Tsvangirai (Hudleston, 2005). Tsvangirai was not gifted with the ability to manage his party or execute transparent and robust decision-making.

A year after the MDC split in 2006, there was much rumour that ZANU-PF was also about to split. Curiously, technocratic vision – precisely a modernisation of the core ZANU-PF nationalist programme, and its re-entry into a modern globalism – was a key issue.

The rumours of a ZANU-PF split were to do, first, with the notion that Solomon and Joice Mujuru, the husband and wife 'power couple' of ZANU-PF, were to demand that Mugabe step down from the party leadership and the national presidency at the September ZANU-PF congress. All 2007, Harare was swept with rumours and counter-rumours as to how much support the Mujurus had. It was not the first time that there had been talk of a party *putsch*. In 2004, the so-called Tsholotsho plotters were meant to have lined up behind Emerson Mnangagwa as successor to Mugabe by making him vice president. The vice presidency instead went to Joice Mujuru. The Mujurus represented an aristocratic generation of military seniority.

Under the name Rex Nhongo, Solomon had commanded Mugabe's guerrilla forces in the liberation struggle and, as Teurai Ropa, Joice had been a genuine war hero, credited with immense courage and prowess. The Mujurus never gathered enough high-level support for their move, and the congress passed without incident – although it is said that Mugabe never forgave Solomon Mujuru for trying. Even so, there had been rumours of a failed military coup earlier that year, involving Mnangagwa – from which he exculpated himself. But Solomon Mujuru never denied he thought it wise for Mugabe to move on. On the eve of the 2013 elections, the viral Facebook character Baba Jukwa claimed that the 2011 death of Solomon Mujuru had been an assassination ordered by Mugabe.

In 2007 the Mujurus had not been seeking the presidency for themselves, but their candidate of choice was Simba Makoni – a technocratic former cabinet minister with responsibilities for financial and economic planning, and known as a person with whom the West would do business, whereas it would not with the sanctioned Robert Mugabe. For months after September, onlookers still wondered whether Makoni would stand for president in the 2008 elections, and whether the Mujurus would still support him. Mugabe was said to have asked Makoni point-blank what his intentions were, and Makoni had assured the old man that he would not be challenged. In the end, Makoni did challenge Mugabe in the presidential race, but the support he hoped would come from the Mujurus never did (Chan, 2007; 2008).

With political and economic instability on his northern frontier, and the possibility of its militarisation and bloodshed, South African president Thabo Mbeki sought to intervene in the Zimbabwean crisis. His view was that a government of unity would help overcome the problems of divisiveness. He cajoled senior figures of both ZANU-PF and the MDC, including Morgan Tsvangirai, to attend a clandestine summit on a houseboat anchored in Lake Kariba. Mbeki's representative who chaired the meeting reportedly confined everyone to the houseboat, having stocked it with large quantities of alcohol, and kept them drinking and talking until the outline of agreement appeared. Constitutional principles were agreed, but the principal innovation was the offer of the vice presidency to Tsvangirai – an offer which flattered Tsvangirai, and one which he was tempted to accept, before finally, after Kariba, declining it. What Kariba did, however, was to give forewarning of how Mbeki saw the Zimbabwean crisis being resolved.

THE 2008 ELECTIONS

That houseboat on Kariba was to haunt Zimbabwe for some years to come, as all discussion on constitutional reform became hinged on how far it departed from what had seemed to emerge as the 'Kariba draft', and what kind of Number Two position could be given to, and exercised by, Morgan Tsvangirai. In a way, the final outcome of the 2008 elections had been conditioned by non-democratic discussions towards the end of 2007. Nevertheless, before that final outcome, the 2008 elections were heavily contested and, from the very first results, it seemed that the MDC might pull off a stunning upset. Inflation, under the ZANU-PF government, had soared to metaphysical levels. Beggars in the streets would throw away bills not denominated in the several million. Restaurants and shops imported Chinese note-counting machines. People carried toiletry bags, if not satchels, of notes to pay for small items. Restaurant tabs changed constantly, and the price for a meal could be very different at the end of the meal from the time when a diner walked in. And that is presuming anything was for sale, in restaurants or supermarkets, anyway. Shortages were an everyday experience and supermarket shelves could be literally empty. The governor of the central bank presided over a quantitative easing that reached an exponential rate, faster than the machines could print new notes.

The 2008 'harmonised elections' were called 'harmonised' because they brought the parliamentary and presidential contests together – and added to them elections for a new senate. They were two years earlier than the end of the parliamentary term (2005–10) and one year later than the end of the presidential term (2002–7), but they were agreed, partly because figures within ZANU-PF itself did not want to lengthen Mugabe's term to 2010 to coincide with the end of parliament's. They reduced the cost and logistics of campaigning and actual polling; but, in addition, they removed opportunities for trials of strength, testing the waters and policies ahead of the next contest; they removed the opportunity to correct electoral rolls, if flawed for one election, in time for the next; and they allowed ZANU-PF a single winner-take-all opportunity to rig a single series of results at a single moment in time.

Moreover, with 2005 changes to the electoral act, pushed through by a ZANU-PF-dominated parliament, for the first time the winner of any presidential election had to receive a majority of the votes, that is, more than 50 per cent. He could not become president by, for example, 49 to 47 per cent. Such a result would mean a run-off. This was to make Tsvangirai's path to victory harder than before and would have made ZANU-PF more confident. The MDC was divided and no grand MDC union occurred, which meant that Arthur Mutambara and Morgan Tsvangirai's parties went head to head. In the presidential race, Mutambara withdrew in favour of Makoni, but ZANU-PF was confident that Makoni had no real party organisation and could not out-campaign Robert Mugabe. Everything looked set for a smooth re-election for Mugabe and his party. ZANU-PF advertising was extremely lacklustre but Tsvangirai's television ads, for the benefit of an urban audience at least, were superb manufactures and examples of advertising agency art.

But the years of meltdown had taken their toll. Notwithstanding the very public fractures in the MDC, the ZANU-PF vote did not come in as the party had expected. The tallies had to be posted outside each polling station and, based on those, Tsvangirai's MDC announced it had achieved 60 per cent of the vote. This was then revised down to 50.3 per cent, as cellphone photographic evidence sent in by party agents was not always clear. South African Broadcasting estimated a 52 per cent MDC victory. One of us (SC) attended these elections and estimated 56 per cent for the MDC – extrapolated from cellphone communications with all key parts of the country, and factoring in historical variables based on ethnicity, population density and past electoral behaviour.

Halfway through counting, the official announcement of results slowed to a crawl. At first the Zimbabwe Electoral Commission had made announcements that Tsvangirai was leading Mugabe two to one in key urban areas. Five days after the election, there was still no announcement of the results, and the ZANU-PF politiburo convened. It would seem that, after a very difficult meeting, the agreement was reached to rig the results. Even so, with the election having been held on 29 March, and the tallies having been posted outside polling stations on 30 March, and the South African Broadcasting estimate having been aired that same night, it took until 2 May before the Electoral Commission gave its results. An assiduous effort had been made to ensure the final results appeared credible. It could not run counter to clear photographic evidence from the polling stations, and so only manipulated what was unclear. It stole from Makoni, as well as from Tsvangirai, in order to build up Mugabe's vote. When the announcement was finally made, Tsvangirai had gained 47.9 per cent, under 50 per cent, and thus had to go into a run-off against Mugabe. Makoni, as the third-place candidate, was eliminated from the run-off to be held on 27 June.

Ferocious violence and intimidation now dominated political life in the electorate. Rigging was followed-up by a simple *force majeure* to coerce from the electorate a vote in favour of Mugabe. The violent coercion became so bad that, just days before the run-off, Tsvangirai withdrew. Mugabe thus went to the polls unopposed, and this time the counting took only two days.

But the national, regional and international furore caused by the nature of Mugabe's victory meant that, once again, South Africa's Thabo Mbeki intervened. He convened the Zimbabwean party leaders under his mediation to find a compromise way forward. He had in mind what he had earlier achieved by way of compromise power-sharing in the Democratic Republic of Congo in 2005, which seemed to end, at least for a time, protracted violent competition (Chan, 2011). He had in mind the coalition government mediated into place by Kofi Annan after the violent Kenyan elections, the outline of a power-sharing formula being announced by Annan on 28 February 2008, a month before Zimbabwe went to the polls. And, of course, Mbeki had in mind the agreement at Kariba towards the end of 2007. Mbeki felt he had momentum to prioritise unity over democracy. It was a choice of values and, for Mbeki, unity and inclusivity were preconditions for any future possibility of mature and functioning democratic practice. Besides, the violence had to end. For South Africa, violent instability on its northern frontier did not bode well. Mbeki was having his own problems keeping the lid on many difficulties back home.

THE GOVERNMENT OF NATIONAL UNITY

To be fair to Thabo Mbeki, whose mediation has been much maligned, he did not face an easy task. Tsvangirai was the electoral victor, but ZANU-PF was clearly unwilling to surrender power. Not only that, but South Africa had expended some energy insisting that the Zimbabwean securocrats should not proceed with a military takeover in the wake of the first round of the elections, before the official results were announced, but when all indications pointed to a change in power. The militarised oligarchy was not going to give in. South Africa did not want to undertake military action, and there had to be genuine doubt as to whether the South African military, now with significant changes in hierarchy and with former ANC generals making a transition from guerrilla to conventional commands, could in fact have overcome a Zimbabwean military blooded from the liberation struggle, and from interventions in Mozambique and the Congo. Mbeki considered negotiation his only option and spent considerable political capital in simply getting the disputants to the table. He also had huge doubts about Tsvangirai's leadership capacity – so, even if all parties accepted a Tsvangirai presidency, would that guarantee stability on South Africa's frontiers, or would a Tsvangirai-led Zimbabwe be chaotic and that chaos spill over the borders? Mbeki had always thought Tsvangirai needed time as a Number Two, before he could become Number One.

More contentiously, Mbeki was committed to his vision of an 'African Renaissance', a renewal, and a stand against the hegemony of the West. So there were two ancillary considerations in Mbeki's mind: Tsvangirai and the MDC's funding from Western sources, and the fact that Mugabe had been a hero of liberation, a hero against white colonial hegemony. It was not just Mbeki. Mugabe's reception by both political figures and the general public in many other African countries suggested how prized his history was – and he and ZANU-PF have always been canny enough to use this. Mbeki's own history has also often been overlooked. Before he became the smooth international face of the ANC-in exile, he too had been trained as a saboteur and fighter. It was Mbeki who taught Zuma how to use an AK47. Mbeki knew how to blow things up; fine suiting was not the only thing he shared with Mugabe.

There was finally the matter of Mugabe's having been sworn in very swiftly after the second round, and his having been acknow-ledged, at an Egyptian meeting of African leaders, as a rightful president. Even so, neither ZANU-PF nor the two MDC parties would have agreed to Mbeki's mediation unless they knew the result was, if not wrong, deeply unsatisfactory and, at least, incredible.

The negotiations were protracted and rancorous. From the end of June, when the second round of the elections had been held, it took two and a half months for a settlement to be agreed. A decisive factor may not have had anything to do with Mbeki, but with Raila Odinga in Kenya, made prime minister as a result of Kofi Annan's work – even though many thought he too had rightly won the presidency. Odinga told Tsvangirai to accept Mbeki's deal, and make it work as Odinga was making his position work in Kenya. Accordingly, Tsvangirai became prime minister to Mugabe's continued presidency. There was no constitutional provision for a prime minister, so this was an

Mbeki invention or gerrymander. There was an MDC majority in both cabinet and parliament (if MDC-Tsvangirai and MDC-Mutambara could cooperate), but it was Mugabe who chaired the cabinet, while Tsvangirai chaired only a council of ministers. In the allocation of ministerial portfolios, ZANU-PF retained control of the security forces. Mugabe also chaired the state security council, on which the powerful generals sat. The ministry of finance went to Tsvangirai's deputy, Tendai Biti. It was to be his unenviable task to stabilise and turn around an economy that was the worst performing in the world.

The cabinet was unwieldy, with 31 ministers, 15 drawn from ZANU-PF, 13 from MDC-Tsvangirai and 3 from MDC-Mutambara. It all represented a balancing act – an inclusive act certainly – but one in which the balance was weighted in security terms towards Mugabe and ZANU-PF, and in which the presidency, despite being stolen, was held by Mugabe. Nevertheless, it gave the MDC some purchase on power. It meant that the political battlefield was now merely political, and would be fought out less on the streets. And it meant the untried Tsvangirai was directly up against Mugabe, one of the wiliest, most experienced politicians of his era. There was a grand ceremony to sign the agreement on 15 September 2008, but arguments about minister-ial portfolios rumbled on until the end of January 2009, and it was only then that Tsvangirai became prime minister.

Mugabe and ZANU-PF thus had enjoyed six months to arrange the political ground as much in their favour as possible. Even so, it did not mean that ZANU-PF welcomed the government of national unity. It accepted grudgingly the GNU, but ZANU-PF knew it had been unprepared for the electoral swing of 2008. It planned to make life hard for Tsvangirai, to depend on him to court international cooper-ation for mending the economy; but to be ready for 2013. It began preparing immediately. Meanwhile, Tsvangirai had to learn the arts of being a prime minister, in political cohabitation with an enemy.

His Western allies did not help beyond a certain point. The greatest accomplishment of the MDC in government was to stabilise the rampantly runaway economy. As minister of finance, Tendai Biti did this by means of a programme of substituting transactable foreign currencies – including the South African rand, but principally the US dollar – for the largely worthless Zimbabwean dollar. Even here, the initial decision to allow other currencies was taken by a ZANU-PF minister during the inter-regnum between the elections and Tsvangirai's becoming prime minister. It was Biti, however, who made it work. The US dollar having value, it meant not so much a rebasing of the currency – the Zimbabwean currency was made redundant – but a rebasing of the economy in terms of true value. US dollars had to be earned and could not be printed. South Africa helped with capital flows and Zimbabwean monies owing to the IMF, and Western countries behind the scenes facilitated some liquidity lines.

However, the West retained sanctions against Mugabe and senior ZANU-PF figures. Although ZANU-PF propaganda has made much of the harmful effects of sanctions, the sanctions in themselves directly affected only a small number of people. What accompanied sanctions, an international disinclination to invest in a sanctioned regime and its perilous economy, caused much more national damage. No foreign direct investment meant no growth was possible for the economy. Lifting the sanctions would have been a signal for re-investment, and the signal throughout Tsvangirai's term never came. But this meant that, although the economy could be stabilised, it could not grow. And, if the West would not lift sanctions and encourage investment for an MDC minister of finance, what was the advantage of having an MDC hand on the economy? It might as well have been a ZANU-PF minister of finance.

On the streets, with the easing of political violence, MDC cadres could gain some hand in community and civic organisation – and also simply in informal street associations, even in youth gangs (Alexander and Chitofiri, 2013). What this did was to encourage ZANU-PF to investigate 'real' electoral campaigning and constituency service. It provided a limit to coercion – which didn't disappear but became more competitive since the 'other side' now also had some power – and this provided an incentive to be seen to be relevant to people's local needs. A rare era of attention to local electoral needs began for ZANU-PF, although this was not always replicated by other parties. Even so, the moment of elections aside, a form of competitive electoral democracy could be discerned in certain urban areas at least.

ZANU-PF worked hard to make Tsvangirai's life difficult, but not impossible. Zimbabwe had to recover from its parlous position – otherwise there would be nothing for which ZANU-PF could claim even partial credit. However Tsvangirai was capable of making his own mistakes. Even though he operated under constrained conditions, he exhibited moments of indecision. No one could ascribe a clear set of policies to him which he could dependably propagate as policies of lasting value.

But two things, in the public perception, took some of the sting out of the politics of this tense cohabitation. The first was that, although he had left ZANU-PF and challenged Mugabe, Simba Makoni was never punished for his desertion, some would say betrayal. He had always been ZANU-PF's technocratic flag-bearer and many in the party still supported a modernised and rationalised nationalisation under a technocratic banner. The second was the sudden death, in a road accident, of Tsvangirai's wife, Susan. This happened on 6 March 2009, shortly after her husband's inauguration as prime minister. It had all the hallmarks of an assassination attempt aimed at the husband. Susan and Morgan Tsvangirai were travelling in the same vehicle when it was struck by a heavy lorry suddenly veering across the road into its path. He survived but she didn't. Afterwards, despite public suspicion, Tsvangirai himself denied it had been anything but a freak accident. The night itself was also marked by the arrival at his hospital bed by Mugabe and his own wife. The television cameras caught Mugabe holding Tsvangirai's hand and muttering over and over again, 'sorry, sorry'. At Susan's funeral, Mugabe's condolences and that of senior ZANU-PF personnel seemed so genuine that Tsvangirai's own son publicly said that he thought real compassion and a desire for cooperation were afoot. Whether they were or not – and it was probably compassion perhaps, but cooperation no – the images of decency and joint sorrow were what inaugurated the GNU. Suddenly the two men, Tsvangirai and Mugabe, seemed like political opponents rather than bitter enemies.

Indeed, from time to time, the two men would make a studied show of public amity, and Tsvangirai would say that he understood and could 'handle' the president. But to what effect? What were the fruits of his premiership? There were certainly some improvements in health provision and social welfare. Agricultural production, including tobacco, improved. But these were not transformative. As much as anything, signs of progress were set against how much more needed to be done to restore Zimbabwe to the levels of productivity and prosperity before the decline of the 2000s. Moreover, despite a combined MDC majority in parliament, there never was a comprehensive nor strategic legislative programme. Parliament sometimes did not sit at all, by agreement of its members, as they agreed to devote the parliamentary budget to their own benefits, for example, in ensuring members had cars.

Certainly Tsvangirai could not say that he successfully required ZANU-PF to fulfil the fine print of the coalition deal. A raft of requirements, under SADC auspices, had been agreed as part of the GNU to ensure a fair playing field for the 2013 elections. These included particularly some dilution of the power of the centralised security system in Zimbabwe. As long as it was ZANU-PF-dominated, it could be used to influence a future election by the application of force. Tsvangirai complained bitterly of this but, shortly after the signing of the accord over the GNU, Mbeki had been recalled from office by his ANC party in South Africa. He was no longer there to police the agreement, and neither his successors nor the SADC as a whole seemed to have the stomach to force Mugabe's hand.

The other major requirement was constitutional reform. This was meant to limit, at least to an extent, the powers of the president. In fact, the final constitutional document which was published in early 2013 still had in place a very powerful president, although it would be fair to say that this was more an African form of French Gaullist president than someone all-commanding. The other two key features of the constitution were in some ways remarkable. The first was a substantial section on human rights, particularly gender rights. Without having the broad range of rights and equalities in the still-unparalleled South African constitution, the Zimbabwean constitution is emphatic and comprehensive about gender rights. The second was the inclusion of 'sunset' clauses which limited presidents to two terms. Here, there were transitional clauses to allow an amelioration of constitutional practice for the first ten years. These transitional clauses were clearly the result of long negotiation and compromise. They applied most tellingly to the question of presidential succession. For the first ten years, a president who retired from office would be replaced, not by parliament or by a vice president, but by someone selected by the outgoing president's political party. This suggested two things: the first was that the ZANU-PF negotiators did not expect Mugabe to remain as president for another ten years; the second was that ZANU-PF saw political power as located within the presidency – even within the slightly scaled-back settlement. ZANU-PF had already learnt to govern in spite of a combined MDC parliamentary majority. It meant that, for the 2013 elections, the important contest would be for president; the parliamentary elections were far less important. If ZANU-PF kept the presidency, the party could command the political landscape, even if the president died in office or retired before the end of his term.

The final constitution had remarkable similarities to the Kariba agreement of 2007. There was no prime ministerial post in it. Any compromise appointments under power-sharing agreements could only be to one of two vice presidential posts – with one able to balance the other out. The constitution was put to referendum in March 2013.

A week before, the Kenyan elections had been held and, in the face of the UN Secretary-General's pleadings that they be 'peaceful and credible', and because neither of the main Kenyan parties wanted to be made to power-share again, and certainly not with the threat of

International Criminal Court sanctions against the planners of violence (Kofi Annan's sting in the tail, which Mbeki had not replicated
in Zimbabwe), the elections were almost soporifically peaceful.
ZANU-PF took note. The international language had mutated from
'free and fair' to 'peaceful and credible'. All it had to do was win the
presidency peacefully and with some credibility. Winning parliament
would be a welcome bonus. Moreover, as incentive, many European
sanctions were lifted at the conclusion of the Zimbabwean referendum – which was in fact conducted freely and fairly, with ZANU-PF
and both MDCs supporting the new constitution.

But, as the time for the elections approached, it seemed apparent that Tsvangirai's MDC was in no hurry for them to occur. It
pleaded to the regional and international community that not all the
Mbeki and SADC conditions to ensure a level playing field, particularly security sector reform, had been achieved. It began to become
apparent that the MDC had recognised how much it now had to lose.
If it lost the elections, Tsvangirai would no longer be prime minister,
there would be no MDC ministers at all and, in the event of yet
another GNU, the new constitution meant that a vice presidency
would be all that could be on offer, and that vice president could not
succeed to the presidency – unless it was the MDC that won outright.
The MDC was suddenly consumed by doubts and ZANU-PF
portrayed this, quite expertly, as the purported democrats suddenly
fighting shy of democracy.

ZANU-PF also thought it had an electoral policy that would be
attractive, and that was extending indigenisation. For a great part of
the 2008–13 period, this had been debated. The broad legislation had
been enacted in 2007, but the detailing became a vexed business. In
essence, the nationalisation of land would be extended to industry and
businesses. Foreign holdings could not exceed 49 per cent. In some
ways, this was a further ransack of the economy. In other ways, it
mirrored policy and practice in even the most dynamic of African
states such as Nigeria, and had been policy at key stages of the
development of South East Asian states and in modern Indonesia.

The key indicator of direction in such policies is whether or not shares awarded to national partners are awarded to individuals or to public concerns. If to individuals, then the creation and enhancement of an oligarchic class would continue apace in Zimbabwe.

The MDC fought these indigenisation policies with a lack both of robustness and imagination. It seemed to accept their inevitability and sought only to negotiate forms of exemption or delay. But, if even the MDC effectively did not oppose indigenisation, and had no significant redistribution policies of its own, then the key policy initiative entering the elections was ZANU-PF's. The incentive for an aspirational voter was to join ZANU-PF and benefit from an indigenisation brought from the countryside to the cities.

3   The Elections of 2013

The decisiveness with which ZANU-PF moved to hold elections was indicative of its confidence and its conviction that the MDC was unprepared. ZANU-PF had been preparing since the settlement that followed the 2008 elections, determined not to share power again. The March referendum on the new constitution was positive, Mugabe signed the constitution into law on 22 May and the elections would be fought under its provisions. The parliamentary term would end on 29 June 2013. Before then, on 31 May, the supreme court, with the end of the parliamentary term in mind, declared that Mugabe had to set a date for the elections, and that the final date on which elections could be called would be 31 July, a month after parliament ended. ZANU-PF then announced that elections would be held for both president and parliament on 31 July.

There was nothing extraordinary in this timing: it would have been normal in normal times. However, Tsvangirai's MDC protested bitterly against the July date, citing in particular the non-completion of all the GNU conditions negotiated under Mbeki, particularly security sector reform. Tsvangirai maintained that, constitutionally, elections did not have to be held until four months after the end of parliament, or until 30 October. There were dangers in this stance, in that it would have left the country effectively under presidential rule for four months, without any check from an MDC-dominated parliament – although, as noted earlier, parliament had hardly checked the president throughout the GNU period.

The MDC was also concerned that ZANU-PF had silently but assiduously 'queered the electoral pitch' by action or inaction on the voters' register. This had in fact been an MDC complaint since 2011, so was not an extemporaneous delaying tactic. There were real grounds for concern about the register: it seemed that one-third of those registered were in fact dead (or otherwise long-lived at up to 120 years of age). The 2013 complaints were about that but also about new young voters not having been registered.

The MDC took its protests to SADC at its summit meeting in Maputo, Mozambique, on 15 June, and SADC recommended an extension until 14 August 2013 – a result greatly heralded by the MDC, although the short delay would have meant little in operational and electoral terms. The issue went to the Zimbabwean supreme court, with even ZANU-PF (somewhat cursorily) pleading for the SADC 14 August date. But the court confirmed 31 July. This was finally accepted by the MDC, with Tsvangirai predicting an historic moment.

The MDC's concern about the register proved well-founded. The electoral rolls were not in fact released until the day before the election – leaving no time for checks and challenges. It seems that there were 100,000 centenarians on the roll – in a country where average life expectancy until that point had been 44. On polling day, the electoral commission reported that 305,000 prospective voters were turned away for not being registered, and 207,000 were 'assisted' in their voting by party agents and officials. Even so, in the presidential race, Mugabe defeated Tsvangirai by 2,110,434 votes (61.09 per cent) to 1,172,349 (34.9 per cent). Even if all the centenarians, unregistered voters and assisted voters had voted for Tsvangirai, Mugabe would still have won. (We refine these figures later in the chapter.) ZANU-PF won 197 parliamentary seats to MDC-Tsvangirai's 70. MDC-Ncube won two. One seat was won by an independent. This left the MDC with less than a third of the parliamentary seats. The MDC petitioned the supreme court, citing irregularities, but then withdrew its suit. Mugabe was sworn in on 22 August, although it took a further three weeks, until 10 September, before he announced his cabinet. Beneath those bald figures, what happened?

THE BUILD-UP AND ITS WARNINGS

To an extent the presidential elections were without charisma. By 2013, both Mugabe and Tsvangirai were well-worn and predictable characters. One could almost script each succeeding line in their campaign speeches. To that extent, despite the crowds, the rallies were set pieces. One MDC figure who had had charisma was Tsvangirai's wife, Susan. During the time Morgan was MDC leader the two lived in an upper-middle class, but far from luxurious, house with gardens and trees – in a respectable but far from top-echelon neighbourhood. She would periodically turn the house into a soup kitchen for the poor. Her generosity was legendary and contrasted with the oligarchic bling-fixation of senior ZANU-PF wives. At rallies, whenever she appeared, the crowds would stand and shout 'Mother! Mother!' at her. Her death removed a vital quality from Tsvangirai's platform – that of acknowledged compassion. Tsvangirai's subsequent move into an expensive prime ministerial residence, the agreement he reached with Mugabe that he could keep the house even if he lost the elections, and the new women in his life – who had none of the compassionate qualities of Susan, and who plied the courts with petitions as to which one was his legitimate new wife – cast a shadow of self-indulgence over his life, where previously there had been an imperfect halo.

This self-indulgence reflected that of others. As early as 2011, the South African commentator Greg Mills described somewhat archly the new love of status symbols on the part of senior MDC officials.[1] For Mills, the MDC had only three choices – to remain within the GNU and fight the subsequent election under SADC rules; to leave the GNU and fight the elections as an opposition party unencumbered by being part of the government – but this would risk losing influence within SADC; or, in the event of a stolen election, to

---

[1] The work and reports of Mills, Booyson, Onslow, International Crisis Group, Zimbabwe Human Rights NGO Forum and others previewed in this section are treated fully and cited in Chapters 6 and 7 of this book.

resort to mass action. Mass action had not worked before. Mills concluded that the MDC remained within the GNU with greed for the benefits of office being a major motivation.

The descent into greed, without the introduction of dynamic new policies that could be identified with the MDC role in govern-ment, meant a huge disappointment for those who had supported Tsvangirai and his party in 2008. A clear warning sign, expressed in the most scientific language possible under Zimbabwean polling con-ditions, was released on 18 August 2012. This was the Freedom House survey of voter intentions conducted from June to July 2012. It was authored by Susan Booysen, a South African academic noted for considerable thoroughness. It surveyed 1,198 people, with a margin of error of 2.8 per cent, at a 95 per cent level of confidence. Such a poll, utilising her methodologies to extract a comprehensive picture of voter intentions and, above all, voter opinions, had never been attempted before in Zimbabwe. Although 47 per cent of respondents declined to declare a voting intention (a figure widely used to discredit or minimise the importance of the survey), Booysen was able to point out that these respondents were 'diffused across party categories' and were, to an extent, comparable to floating voters in the surveys preceding metropolitan elections. In other words, even those with previous party affiliations were prepared to wait and see, and judge, on performance and persuasion factors as the full term of government expired and the election commenced. In short, the 47 per cent represented an 'everything to play for' factor.

Having said that, her other figures were alarming for the MDC, and encouraging for ZANU-PF. The MDC had, from 2010 to 2012, dropped in popularity from 38 to 20 per cent – whereas ZANU-PF had risen in popularity from 17 to 31 per cent. 52 per cent trusted ZANU-PF, whereas only 39 per cent trusted the MDC.

Particularly telling was Booysen's comment that all respond-ents 'speak the same political and economic language ... especially in the experience of economic issues, and often in the assessment of government'. This would suggest at least a level of class cohesion in her respondents and, given the complex range of questions put by the survey, the respondents were also likely to have been well educated. Supposing a significantly middle-class group of respondents, the battle for the floating voter was likely to be within the middle class – speaking with the 'same political and economic language', and having the same economic and political expectations. We will argue that these expectations were growth and stability.

The MDC was alarmed by the survey – but did nothing to remedy its image or its underlying faults. Neither did it begin to strategise how to capture the 47 per cent. The MDC seemed to put its faith in an historic moment – in which the voters would move away from ZANU-PF – and in SADC. The conviction was that SADC, as custodians of the Mbeki conditions, would demand, then guarantee, security sector reform. With that sector reformed, or at least more pluralistically populated, ZANU-PF could not win on a fear factor Ascribing only a fear factor to ZANU-PF was a mistake. Relying on SADC was another.

As early as 2011, the London School of Economics scholar Sue Onslow had categorically predicted that SADC would not move forcibly against ZANU-PF. In an extensive argument, she cited the levels of support for ZANU-PF within SADC; but also the military inability of the SADC countries, including South Africa, to challenge Zimbabwe; and the very diffuse nature of economic sanctions, if ever they were applied. The one success of SADC has been to create progress on regional economic integration, and so no country could sanction Zimbabwe without harming its own economy. In reality, SADC had little leverage – it had no silver bullet – but MDC expectation was that, somehow, a silver bullet was available.

The prospect of ZANU-PF's calling SADC's bluff became clear in a SAPES Policy Forum debate between two ministers, Patrick Chinamasa of ZANU-PF and Tendai Biti of the MDC, in Harare in May 2012. Biti insisted that the date for the next election could only be agreed in concert with the SADC facilitator – meaning South African President Zuma – but Chinamasa, almost chillingly, said the elections would be held 'sooner rather than later', and would be an internal matter – no matter what SADC said.

It indeed seemed not to matter what SADC said. The 9 March 2013 report by President Zuma to the SADC Organ Troika on Politics, Defence and Security Cooperation made several 'extremely urgent' recommendations for security sector reform in Zimbabwe, to secure confidence in the elections. A June SADC meeting made similar calls – and these calls had no effect. Indeed in June it seemed that ZANU-PF had moved senior military officers into key rural areas. Even if they were not there to organise intimidation or suppression, they certainly gave an edge to electoral strategy at local levels. On the very eve of elections, 30 July, the SAPES Policy Dialogue Forum categorically stated that key SADC conditions had not been met.

The date of 31 July for the elections had been achieved by a curious judicially based stratagem. In May, a court action was brought by Jealousy Mbizvo Mawarire, in his self-declared capacity as a private citizen (although it was rumoured he was a CIO agent), and he demanded of the leading figures of the government, including both Mugabe and Tsvangirai, that his right as a citizen to know the date of the election should be honoured. The case was heard on 24 and 31 May, one month before the end of the parliamentary term, and the court – in a contentious ruling that nevertheless utilised a reasonable disquisition on electoral law – declared a latest election date of 31 July. The MDC seemed stunned by this development and, as noted earlier, its appeals to SADC were unsuccessful. Recourse to SADC having failed, the MDC had no choice but to fight the elections. As it turned out, the security sector did not use a heavy hand upon the electoral process – not as far as intimidation was concerned. The levels of physical violence were very substantially less than in the second 2008 round and accorded with the level of peacefulness found earlier in 2013 in Kenya. That seemed to have become a litmus test even for the Zimbabwean security forces. In early May, the opinion of the International Crisis Group (ICG) was that the MDC was not ready for an election. Its 6 May report listed many faults of cohesion and capacity.

On the eve of the elections, the ICG issued a further, pessimistic report on how well democracy would be served by the elections, as, at the same time, did the South African-based Solidarity Peace Trust. In a full-page newspaper advertisement, the Zimbabwe Lawyers for Human Rights protested the timing of the election but urged a 'responsible' vote. Transparency International Zimbabwe took out a similar full-page urging a peaceful vote for 'personal convictions'. The polls went ahead with a result many anticipated and dreaded. Both the MDC and many civic action groups had indicated huge flaws in the electoral process, so that their condemnations afterwards seemed like prophecies fulfilled. The reasons for defeat were rehearsed from the outset. It was an election of superficial dynamism. The crowds for both parties were stunning and vibrant; this time, ZANU-PF media advertisements were glossy and immaculate and outshone those of the MDC; and smartphones relayed news of what was happening from one end of the country to the other. But it was also an election of a curious negativity and resignation on the part of the MDC. A smug Mugabe took an almost cat-like satisfaction in charming a foreign press contingent with its usual impersonations of hard-bitten swagger.

THE DAY OF 31 JULY

On the day of polling, the independent *Daily News* led on its front page with '89 reasons why Mugabe must go'.[2] In fact, there were only 60 reasons, but the 89 referred to his age. ZANU-PF was also aware of the age, vigour and technocratic-awareness issue – but that was not an issue for Mugabe's party at this election. It would resonate afterwards. In the same edition, Mugabe said he would accept defeat: 'If you lose you must surrender to those who have won.'[3] This followed what was reported as a 'jovial' meeting between Mugabe, Tsvangirai, and former Nigerian president Olusegun Obasanjo, head of the African Union observers. Tsvangirai, for his part, contributed an article to the edition, calling once again for an historical 'single defining moment'.[4]

[2] *Daily News*, 31 July 2013: 1 & 4.   [3] Ibid: 8.   [4] Ibid: 9.

Baba Jukwa, with 302,403 Facebook followers, advised his fans and followers to vote for Tsvangirai.[5] The next day's *Daily News* edition of 1 August was already talking of massive fraud in a high turnout – although no real figures of votes cast or overall turnout had yet been made clear.[6] But, on 3 August, the day after results began to flow in, with trends already clear, the newspaper led with Tsvangirai's angry denunciation of the polls as a 'huge farce'.[7] The independent Zimbabwe Election Support Network (ZESN), with 7,000 independent Zimbabwean observers drawn from civil society and local communities, said 'all is not well'. But its preliminary report, although observant of many irregularities on polling day, concentrated on what it called 'disenfranchisement' – with a large number unable to vote because of not having been entered on the voters' register.[8]

The accounts released by the Zimbabwe Human Rights NGO Forum on 1 August stated that an estimated 761,689 people eligible to be registered had not been. However, registration had been markedly different in town and countryside. In the rural areas, 99.7 per cent of the eligible voters had been registered, whereas in urban areas the figure was only 67.94 per cent. This was before either official trends or results were announced and, as noted earlier, there was an element of getting one's excuses in ahead of time.

In the event, Mugabe defeated Tsvangirai by 938,085 votes (2,110,434 to 1,172,349) – so that, if all the unregistered eligibles (761,689 including the 305,000 turned away on the grounds of not having been registered) and those, such as the elderly or illiterate who were assisted to vote by party agents or officials (207,000), had voted for Tsvangirai, then Tsvangirai would have defeated Mugabe by 30,604 votes. If all the centenarians (100,000) were assumed to have voted for Mugabe, and then discounted as manufactured votes, the Tsvangirai margin of victory would have been 130,604. But it is highly unlikely, given the Booysen Freedom House survey, that all such

[5] Ibid.   [6] *Daily News*, 1 August 2013:1–2.
[7] *Daily News*, 3 August 2013:1.   [8] Ibid: 4.

votes would have gone to Tsvangirai. Even without discounting the centenarians, which is a problematic sector as we do not know how many voted and whether they would have been double-counted among those assisted to vote because of infirmities, and given Booysen's survey results, even the most optimistic estimates would not have had Tsvangirai capturing enough of the disputed votes and eligible votes-that-never-were to defeat Mugabe – although the result would have been somewhat closer.

Six months before the elections, one of us (SC) met with the three key ambassadors to Zimbabwe – the US, UK and Australian (the last because he was chair of the 'Fishmongers' group, the Western ambassadors who regularly met at the restaurant of that name). Using the Booysen results and their own extrapolations, they calculated that, in a straight fight between Mugabe and Tsvangirai, and in a free and fair contest, Mugabe could still win by 54 per cent.[9] However, given the state of the voting register, and given that the MDC had not, and seemed to have no plans to mount a concerted registration drive, it seemed that ZANU-PF was able to pin many of its hopes on a favourable or 'conditioned' register. This accords with ZESN's eve-of-results verdict that the register was a lead consideration in the forthcoming results. On that basis, this all suggested that ZANU-PF was hoping for a 62 per cent presidential result.

Mugabe in the end won 61.9 per cent. The parliamentary results were also pleasing for ZANU-PF, with the MDC falling under one-third of the total seats. There were instances of local malpractice, including 'bussing' of voters (mass transport to polling stations of 'voters' with dubious registration credentials) being observed particularly in some urban constituencies. It is impossible to state categorically whether, and how much, this occurred nationally. The parliamentary figures, which were higher than those for the president, flattered ZANU-PF, and this would have been a bonus for a strategy

[9] This figure was based on the absence of Ncube as an MDC vote-divider and spoiler. In the event, however, Ncube attracted a small fraction of the vote.

that had prioritised the presidential poll. Under the new constitution, its two-thirds majority put the presidential succession in the hands of ZANU-PF. ZANU-PF might have managed without the two-thirds majority, but the party had clearly believed the Booysen figures and worked hard on the 47 per cent of floating voters.

The African Union and SADC observer teams, with some caveats and misgivings, broadly accepted the results and were glad to get out of the country and hope for a less troublesome region with an undisputed government in Zimbabwe. That undisputed government had, in the parliamentary vote, seen not only the diminution of MDC strength, but the decimation of the MDC front bench. One by one, Tsvangirai's lieutenants fell.

How did they do it? Why did so many voters turn to ZANU-PF and Robert Mugabe; why did they do so in formerly staunchly anti-ZANU-PF parts of the country like Matabeleland? The next two chapters explore these questions from the perspectives of grass-roots activists and ordinary voters.

4   'We Are Tired of Supporting a Loser'

The MDC Campaign

After its historic electoral success in 2008 and four years serving inside government, rather than battling it from the outside, many in the MDC appeared to believe that outright victory was within reach. By August 2013, the party was having to come to terms with a dramatic reversal in fortune. This chapter and the next describe how Zimbabwean voters explain this.

The accounts offered here are based on interviews carried out with political party activists from both MDC parties and ZANU-PF, as well as civil society and community activists.[1] Because most of these interviews took place three months after the elections, as the country was still digesting the outcome, much of the thinking expressed was under development: these were some of the first opportunities for grass-roots activists to air and develop a verdict on what had happened. As a result, group interviews took very different dynamics. One group of MDC loyalists in Chitungwiza, a dormitory town some 30 km south of Harare, appeared stupefied by the outcome. Crowded into the local party chairman's small, dark sitting room, they asked for help. 'Tell us how to get rid of this man [Mugabe], we have tried everything and failed.'[2] This group were unable to understand the election outcome as anything other than stolen. Another group, a mixture of MDC-T and MDC-N activists in Bulawayo, gathered in the 12th floor office of a sympathetic civil society organiser (arriving in various states of exhaustion, the lift being broken). Although the meeting began with attempts to defend the MDCs, and to emphasise

---

[1] We have tended to use loose, generic terms to describe each interviewee, usually those suggested by interviewees themselves. Where names have been used these have been changed. Exact organisation names and locations have not been given.

[2] MDC activists, Chitungwiza, 3 November 2013 (JG).

the role of rigging in achieving a victory for ZANU-PF, it quickly transformed into an account of drastic failure and disillusion within the opposition parties. Other groups were more cautious, like the group of urban market traders who gathered in the offices of local union officials. Scattered around the edge of the room as if trying to spread as far apart from each other as possible, members of the group were reluctant to talk and refused outright to discuss politics. Some opened up in one-to-one encounters afterwards, explaining that in a group they all felt it was safer to avoid politics. None of the members of this group had voted. Even more cautious were the voters in the ZANU-PF stronghold Mashonaland Central who were interviewed under cover at an NGO office in a dusty growth point, arriving ostensibly to meet its head, and then slipping into a backroom to be interviewed.

The fracture and chaos in the elite levels of the MDC following the election rested on equally disjointed thinking in the lower levels. Criticism and despair spilled out from every direction. The analysis that follows reflects the sense that many MDC activists expressed of relief at finally being able to vent their frustration, and their inability to see a constructive future for the party that had once come so close to ending Mugabe's rule.

In total 69 people were interviewed in this November visit. Each was asked to 'tell the story of the election', and left to define the key elements for themselves. There were different emphases across the country, and we will outline these as they arise. But overall, four main features were used to describe the MDC failure in 2013. First, their party structures and relationships were weak and fractious; second, it became clear during this election that their relationship with the electorate was built on shaky foundations; third, their performance in government played against them; and fourth, they ran a disastrously disorganised campaign.

PARTY RELATIONSHIPS AND STRUCTURES

Local activists felt excluded and unsupported in 2013, and as a result there was far less enthusiasm for the election than in previous campaigns. One MDC-T activist who campaigned in a rural part of Matabeleland South complained that the leaders had become 'too important' to muck in with their comrades.

> We used to travel with these guys using worn out old cars, sleeping in huts. Now they are rich, they are too special. They used to have meetings under trees. Now they are complaining that it is too hot.[3]

Once they had caught their breaths, the MDC activists arriving at the 12th floor Bulawayo offices began a heated debate, almost a competition to see who could apportion the most blame. They described how a culture of suspicion had developed over the GNU period.

> When these guys went into government, you could meet in the road and speak. Now these guys are MPs, you meet and you are pushed. They use the CIO [Central Intelligence Organisation] as their aids and they are spying on us.
>
>   The MDC was supposed to be pro-poor but when people got into power they got cars and there was a dividing line between them and their people. They adopted the chefdom mentality. But in our democracy we believe issues should be discussed so there was a rift between the leadership and the members. They don't have time to talk to old comrades anymore.[4]

Party activists and civil society leaders were in despair over the opposition parties' poor organisation. The two MDCs' inability to form a coalition was seen as disastrous – as many pointed out, how could they be expected to run a country when they couldn't even pull together to oppose ZANU PF? Instead, the party had devoted its energies to time-consuming and damaging internal battles.

Eric is an MDC-T loyalist who failed to get through a bruising selection process to run as a candidate for his local council. He has

---

[3] MDC-T activist, Matobo, 10 November 2013 (JG).
[4] MDC-N activists, Bulawayo, 9 November 2013 (JG).

been a branch chairman and a keen campaigner from the early days of the party's formation. He and members of his family lived through the worst of the violence: his home has been ransacked by the police and he and his wife have both been badly beaten. Now he watches as what he sees as inexperienced candidates are preferred.

> People thought they had won when they had not, so we spent too much energy on internal selection. This was marred, it wasn't as transparent as it should have been. We have the youth and women empowerment policies which were not refined properly. The youth want 50 per cent and the women want 50 per cent, and what do the men get? People were working against each other. There was a lot of disgruntlement – those best suited often didn't get the posts.[5]

Instead, activists who had been living abroad and were seen as out of touch returned to be given priority, along with young candidates, women, family members, old friends – all seemed to be favoured over local activists. As another MDC-T activist said: 'They would bring someone from the UK two weeks before the election.'

This left many activists – the people the parties needed to run election campaigns – bitter and disillusioned; and it played badly with the electorate who saw a disunited, incompetent opposition, fielding lightweight or corrupt candidates. Local MDC activists in Matabeleland could see all too well how corrupt selection procedures played with the voters: 'We went with our thieves to the electorate; ZANU got rid of theirs.'[6] A CSO organiser, once a sympathiser of the MDC said:

> The MDC was unable to select candidates, to identify its real cadres from the opportunists ... Instead of fighting against Mugabe, the MDC guys were fighting against Tsvangirai.[7]

---

[5] MDC activist, Chitungwiza, 3 November 2013 (JG).
[6] MDC-N activist, Bulawayo, 9 November 2013 (JG).
[7] CSO leader, Harare, 4 November 2013 (JG).

The MDC activists in the 12th floor Bulawayo office became more and more angry as they reflected on the effects of the internal battles. They were particularly disturbed by the failure of the two MDC parties to form an electoral pact, a failure that helped hand electoral victory to Mugabe:

> We have been talking about a dictatorship in Zimbabwe but I believe the worst dictators are in the MDCs. You cannot find Mugabe imposing a candidate. But Morgan [Tsvangirai] and Welshman [Ncube] don't want to devolve power.
>
> People formed the GNU to reform problems but instead they went back to internal fights. Morgan and Welshman were supposed to reconcile and fight for the people of Zimbabwe but they went back to fight each other.
>
> And Mugabe was a free man.[8]

RELATIONSHIPS WITH THE ELECTORATE

Poor relationships within the party spilled over into the support-base and wider electorate. This was exacerbated by a less clear electoral choice – now voters contemplated the differences between two parties in power, both more or less corrupt and remote.

The MDC was established on a trade union base, which had gradually expanded to bring in civil society and support from the poor urban areas. It also had early on won the backing of much of the white farming community – a source of financial help, but also a problematic association for the party.

As LeBas (2011) has argued, the MDC built its support base within a starkly polarised political climate. As it emerged, the party deliberately highlighted the differences between it and ZANU-PF as a way to build loyalty and make the idea of shifting allegiance unthinkable to supporters. LeBas details the ways in which

---

[8] MDC-N activists, Bulawayo, 9 November 2013.

polarisation was entrenched through violent confrontation, a mechanism which emphasised the unbridgeable gulf between the parties – and several of the MDC activists interviewed expressed regret that politics had become so calm – for many it had lost its urgency and its edge. Polarisation was also based on apparently clear-cut ideological differences. The MDC projected itself as a liberal party that prioritised human rights and democracy, and it empha-sised its relationships with Western well-wishers and financial backers. ZANU-PF meanwhile prioritised a form of nationalism shaped on a repudiation of colonial history, an identification of Zimbabweanness rooted in the land, and articulated in confronta-tional standoffs with the country's white farmers and the West (Ndlovu-Gatsheni 2009; Tendi, 2010).

However, as LeBas (2014) argues, the GNU whittled away this polarisation. As a partner in government, the MDC lost its ability to mark itself out as antithetical to ZANU-PF, and forfeited the solidity of its hold on its supporters. Moreover, it became clear that many MDC MPs slipped into some of the methods and approaches to gov-ernment that had once seemed the sole preserve of ZANU-PF, losing touch with constituents and appearing to focus on acquiring material benefits for themselves instead of pursuing national priorities. As one civil society activist put it:

> The guys from the MDC won their constituencies and left them and didn't care. When people begin to assume national priorities they forget their local priorities.[9]

Certainly, during the GNU period the party had put far less energy into shoring up its support. Tsvangirai had moved away from the ZCTU, which at the same time had suffered through the dramatic fall in formal sector jobs. As a result, many felt that the party had become doubly removed from its core.

---

[9] CSO leader, Bulawayo, 8 November 2013 (JG).

When you are a labour party, you mustn't forget your people in labour. You need to support industry. They would blame the MDC for not doing that. Workers were agitated because they felt they were getting too little.[10]

Trade union activists felt particularly keenly that the party identity had been diluted.

Tsvangirai moved away from the ZCTU, along the way there were people who were not trade unionists that came and joined. That's where he made a big mistake. This was supposed to be a labour party. It was formed to advance the interests of the poor. Then when some powerful guys – black and white – came to support, that's when he lost support [of his base]. He said the MDC was an omnibus, anyone could come and join. So he lost focus of why the party was formed. This party was supposed to push for the working people's agenda. But the people still support him – at least for now. He should come back to the people.[11]

This underlines the shallowness of the MDC's support base. Two CSO activists who had been sympathetic towards the party now pointed to the flimsiness of the MDC connection with the electorate. The first works with farmers out of a tiny, asbestos-roofed office in rural Mashonaland; the second with residents in urban Bulawayo. But both described a similar story.

People support the MDC as an alternative, rather than as an ideal political party. If another party with better policies and ideals [came along], I think people would go for that. Some people disapproved of the MDC going into the unity government – they saw it as a betrayal. Most of them did not vote, they were so frustrated.[12]

The opposition offers nothing tangible or 'ideal' ... It did not have loyal members that were sold into the cause ... ZANU-PF has got

---

[10] Teacher, Old Pumula, 9 November 2013 (JG).
[11] Trade unionist, Harare, 15 November 2013 (JG).
[12] Agricultural advisor, Mashonaland Central, 14 November 2013 (JG).

supporters and the opposition has got sympathisers. Supporters are loyal – even if things are going wrong they will continue to support. They contribute to the party. They believe in the cause. And the MDC has sympathisers – disgruntled ZANU-PF people, with scores to settle, opportunists. Some are genuine activists. There is no ideological connection between the sympathisers and the MDC. They are more fluid. You can't count on them. They can abandon the ship.[13]

And even party loyalists had begun to argue that MDC support was a product of desperation rather than deep ideological connection. One MDC-N activist said: 'In 2008 a lot of people voted MDC because of hunger. It was hunger.'[14]

Lovemore runs a community support group from a Harare office, working with some of Harare's poorest inhabitants as they struggle to cope with brutal living conditions. Residents from Mbare and Highfield, areas which were once bulldozed by state forces, and now house families squeezed into poor-quality tenement buildings, sometimes as many as 15 to a room, traipse out to the office in a tree-lined street, to discuss problems with sewage and rubbish, electricity bills and rent demands. Lovemore said that he had been desperate in the past to see the opposition succeed but now he has no time for Tsvangirai and the rest of the MDC leadership, which he sees as no better or even worse than ZANU-PF. One of the problems, he explained, was the way in which the 'chefdom mentality' had gone to the heads of the MDC leadership:

> One of the weaknesses of the MDC is the glory-seeking nature of their leadership. They think everything revolves around them.... In Harare most people are concerned with the attitude of the MDC – they think they have become arrogant and self-serving and are opportunists.[15]

[13] CSO leader, Bulawayo, 11 November 2013 (JG).
[14] MDC-N activist, Bulawayo, 9 November 2013 (JG).
[15] CSO leader, Harare, 4 November 2013 (JG).

PERFORMANCE IN GOVERNMENT

There was a strong sense, particularly in MDC-strongholds, that as soon as the party went into the government it was to be held to account. Rather than being seen as junior coalition partners, the parties were viewed as fully in power. This effect was most marked in Matabeleland where the MDC was often viewed as the only party in power (the region having returned no ZANU-PF MPs in 2008). The following four comments express this: the first two are from a priest and a teacher, men who both work with some of the poorest people in peri-urban areas around Bulawayo. The third and fourth are from an MDC activist and sympathetic CSO activist, who likewise realise the sense of disappointment arising from the failure of the MDC parties in government.

> What was promised, even by the MDC was not delivered. Many people did not vote because they don't see any change ... There is a change since 2008. Then people had that hope that the MDC was going to win. Then when it didn't happen, people lost interest.[16]

> Most people, once they have been disappointed in the GNU, they felt they were being left out. Very few people were pretty comfortable but the majority didn't get much. A lot of people felt we have given you a chance, but it's still sliding down the scale so the best thing is to return that person who brought us independence and let him try again.[17]

> People for that five-year period, people were assessing, what has this person done for us? He just wanted to get rich. People now would be wanting someone who would bring development to the community.[18]

> Where people lost [their seats], it was sitting MPs. Mainly they lost because people were sick of them. You have a spotlight as a sitting MP. Residents expect you to do something for them.[19]

---

[16] Priest, Emganwini township, 12 November 2013 (JG).
[17] Teacher, Old Pumula, 9 November 2013 (JG).
[18] MDC-T activists, Matobo, 10 November 2013 (JG).
[19] CSO leader, Bulawayo, 8 November 2013 (JG).

Some activists were aggrieved that the MDC got the blame for every-thing, even though they were relatively junior partners in the GNU. One MDC loyalist complained: 'And even potholes [get called] MDC potholes: everything which is wrong is attributed to the MDC.'[20] But even this activist, and the colleague who was interviewed alongside him, admitted that many MDC politicians had been not only incom-petent, but corrupt. These two MDC loyalists live in Chitungwiza, controlled by the MDC council, and where high levels of corruption over access to plots for housing had led to the arrest and imprison-ment of the councillor responsible for housing. This was an important factor in the loss of seven council seats in 2013, and also affected the loss of local parliamentary seats, they admitted.

> The MDC problem was while the MDC was in the IG [Inclusive Government] in charge of towns, it let its councillors get so corrupt. They were selling [housing] stands for $5,000 – they would pay $200 to the council and pocket the rest. They were shooting themselves in the foot.[21]

This story played out on a national scale too, where arguments about corruption exacerbated splits within the party. A CSO activist described how his organisation's questioning of MDC probity led to a breach of confidence.

> Some MDC guys received $50,000 development funds. You could see the next constituency being developed and not yours. We asked the MDC guys, where is development? And we had a serious problem – there was war in Bulawayo. They said, you guys are ZANU. They didn't like that because a number of MPs were taking the money.[22]

One locally employed official working for a European embassy pointed out that corruption and arrogance in power was not exclusive

---

[20] MDC-T supporter, Chitungwiza, 3 November 2013 (JG).

[21] MDC activists, Chitungwiza, 3 November 2013 (JG).

[22] CSO leader, Bulawayo, 8 November 2013 (JG).

to the MDC – 'so what? ZANU-PF are far worse', he said.[23] Yet for many voters it appears that there was a difference. The MDC's appeal was rooted in the idea of its differences from ZANU-PF, one of which was the idea of probity in government. The loss of that difference was treated by many as a betrayal of the wider project.

The experience of the GNU weakened faith in the MDC parties. Many voters felt in 2012 that the MDC either could not, or would not, deliver any change.

> People feel powerless when they vote but nothing changes.[24]
>
> The politicians have failed the people. All parties have failed – they are in it for the money.[25]

One of the most troubling problems for MDC members and supporters was the performance of their leader. Before the GNU period, Morgan Tsvangirai was largely well-respected. The beatings and detention, smear campaigns and charges of corruption he was subjected to, and perhaps most dramatically his refusal to make a political issue over the death of his wife in a car accident in still-unclear circumstances, are often cited as examples of his personal bravery. Questions over his lack of decisiveness, his judgement and his political skill are admitted, even by some of his staunchest supporters, but until the GNU period, these were usually forgiven.[26] One very loyal MDC member said:

> That guy, OK, he is not as well-educated, but he has got the calibre and the guts to face that bull. He is the only man who can stare ZANU-PF in the eye.[27]

For people who have felt intimidated into silence, this is a particularly important quality. A headmaster who is based in Mashonaland

---

[23] Locally employed official in a European embassy, Harare, 6 November 2013 (JG).

[24] CSO leader, Bulawayo, 11 November 2013 (JG).

[25] Informal trader, Bulawayo, 12 November 2013 (JG).

[26] Trade unionist, Harare, 5 November 2013.

[27] MDC-T activist, Chitungwiza, 3 November 2013.

Central explained how he is forced to host ZANU-PF meetings in his school; 'but I can never allow the other side to come and do similar things'. He spoke nervously: 'If you use my name you will find me [makes cutting motion on his neck].' For this man, and others like him, Tsvangirai's courage is inspirational.

> They uphold Morgan Tsvangirai as someone who is very brave. No one else has ever challenged the government up to the levels that gentleman reached. He has never given up. They view him as courageous.[28]

However, weaknesses in an opposition leader proved less tolerable in a prime minister. Many observers felt that Tsvangirai was left with less authority after his period as prime minister. This tone was particularly noticeable in Matabeleland. A priest from Old Pumula outside Bulawayo pointed to the feeling of many that Tsvangirai had shown himself to be ineffective in government.

> [T]he MDC is not a good alternative. He is not competent, he gives conflicting theories of the MDC. Morgan Tsvangirai, it was OK for him at the beginning but now there is need for new ideas. It is high time for someone new. Soon there will be no difference between him and the president.[29]

One CSO leader in Bulawayo also highlighted the disappointment felt at Tsvangirai's performance in government:

> Tsvangirai was the alternative father-figure. He had stayed for some time and he had begun to enjoy that position. Meanwhile ZANU delivered.[30]

Another civil society leader who organised a meeting between the MDC leader and voters in Bulawayo described his despair about the way Tsvangirai managed to alienate people.

---

[28] Head teacher, Mashonaland Central, 14 November 2013 (JG).

[29] Priest, Emganwini township, 12 November 2013 (JG).

[30] CSO leader, Bulawayo, 11 November 2013 (JG).

We called Tsvangirai to a meeting with civil society in Bulawayo and it was a disaster. People said, there might be a problem with people not having washed because we have a water shortage here. He laughed and said, why not use perfume? Somebody said, we have not been getting our salaries and he laughed ... He needs to deal with that issue, but instead he laughed ... The man was crying.[31]

Alongside Tsvangirai's apparent enjoyment of his comfortable government position were the many stories of his colourful love life including a string of glamorous girlfriends, paternity suits and eventually a lavish wedding. His lack of restraint was described by some as a lapse of judgement, and others an outright lack of moral fibre. One MDC stalwart said:

He is not corrupt. He makes stupid moves – in his love for women – but he is straight.[32]

More critical comments included:

The public perception on Tsvangirai was very weak. He had been bedding a lot of women and has been very inconsistent. I would not vote for a president who sleeps around.[33]

Morgan, the issue of women. He paid a lot of money for those [paternity] cases. Where did he get that money from?[34]

He was a womaniser – he was not leading by example. People didn't like that.[35]

The image of Tsvangirai somehow tarnished ... We had people who were ready to die for Tsvangirai, but now they are talking of someone else.[36]

[31] CSO leader, Bulawayo, 8 November 2013 (JG).
[32] MDC-T supporter, Chitungwiza, 3 November 2013 (JG).
[33] CSO leader, Harare, 4 November 2013 (JG).
[34] MDC-T activist, Matobo, 10 November 2013 (JG).
[35] Village headman, Matobo, 10 November 2013 (JG).
[36] NGO worker, Mashonaland Central, 14 November 2013 (JG).

Many party activists voiced frustration. As they discussed the problems of leadership, the MDC group in Bulawayo began to express their despair at the prospects for their parties.

> We are losing faith in the leaders – Welshman and Morgan. They are fighting their personal wars.
> We need a completely new party. I condemn all our leaders.
> People are scattered. They have lost confidence.
> If we are not careful, we will lose even more in 2018.[37]

THREE BIG PROBLEMS WITH THE CAMPAIGN

Phillan Zamchiya, who spent the election campaign with the MDC-T leadership, highlights a number of crucial problems. He described how Tsvangirai's close advisors refused to listen to advice from the party's technical team which warned of the structural and ideological challenges that would make a victory difficult for the party. They did not believe the naysayers because they were 'blinded by ambition, suspicion of intellectuals, the animated atmosphere at political rallies, and a creeping sense of a divine ordination to govern' (Zamchiya, 2013: 956). Zamchiya also pointed to the shortage of funds for the campaign – just US$100 for each council candidate and US$1,400 for each parliamentary candidate, with one car allocated to cover each province, meant to service around 20 parliamentary seats (Ibid.: 961). These sums were trifling compared to ZANU-PF's substantial campaign chest. A further problem was the party's failure to present an ideologically resonant message, in particular because it chose to ignore the issues of indigenisation, sanctions and the independence struggle, leaving Mugabe to claim the important mantle of liberation leader (Ibid.: 958).

These problems were viewed very clearly – if slightly differently – from the vantage point of the voters. What Zamchiya calls the 'divine right to govern' was seen as complacency. The lack of

---

[37] MDC activists, Bulawayo, 9 November 2013 (JG).

resources was viewed as part of a general tendency towards incompetence and selfishness, seen in particular among party faithful as a failure to plan an effective campaign. Most clear of all was the party's inability to create a policy platform that resonated with voters.

A huge problem with the election campaign, according to activists, was complacency. The party leadership appeared to feel that there was no need to campaign because all it needed was one more push to dislodge ZANU-PF. They imagined they could rely on their support from 2008, and, without the violence that had characterised that election, they would be home and dry. As a result, they neglected the central issue of voter registration. The teacher in Old Pumula saw how this failure led to the effective disenfranchisement of many voters.

> The MDC was busy preaching the gospel of change rather than focusing on registration. So they had the support of the masses, but most are not registered. Also, many MDC voters have left the country. Most supporters are sympathisers, not voters.[38]

And the priest also fell victim to this problem. Having tried to persuade his congregation to use their votes, he found himself driving around trying to do so himself.

> When I went to vote I did not find my name. So I had to go back to my old constituency. [There] I found my parents who are both late [dead] and all my brothers who are not in Zimbabwe, on the roll ... I did not manage to vote – my name was not there.[39]

All this was seen as part of the problem of complacency. The MDC took its support for granted; its leaders did not think they needed to make an effort to woo voters:

> We have a political party without a strategy which just counted on ZANU-PF failing ... The MDC assumed people are reasonable, they

---

[38] Teacher, Old Pumula, 9 November 2013 (JG).
[39] Priest, Emganwini township, 12 November 2013 (JG).

will vote MDC. But they forgot, you went into government and you
failed the people. Meanwhile ZANU-PF were out with the people
and helping people.[40]

Matabeleland, a region the MDC thought it could count on, appears to
have suffered a particularly acute shortage of resources. The region is
thinly populated, with large constituencies, making the shortage of
transport a devastating problem. Two MDC-T activists in Motobo in
Matabeleland, an area of great beauty and severe poverty, described
how badly organised the campaign itself was. One man, who described
himself as a 'roving polling agent', said it was virtually impossible to
do his job. His frustration had led him and his colleague to question
the probity of the party leadership:

> [T]he MDC failed to pay the polling agents. Why? Some of the
> polling agents can change at any time if you don't pay them. I was
> out in the field for six weeks but I got nothing from the party. I had
> to find [money] myself ... Why is the party not coming with
> resources? All the parties were given money by the government, the
> treasury. If they don't have money then where do they get money
> for these expensive cars?
>
> People are not sure if it's the MP who took the money of this
> roving guy so this chases people away.
>
> ZANU-PF gave the candidates brand new vehicles.
>
> Before the inclusive government, polling agents were given food
> packs and money – in 2008 it was better organised.
>
> Now it's difficult for anyone to persuade me to go anywhere.
> I want cash upfront.
>
> People said, if you don't give us some money we'll quit. I was
> using my own car to campaign – the party did not provide one.
> Some of the leadership abused funds ... I am even thinking of
> quitting.[41]

---

[40] CSO leader, Bulawayo, 8 November 2013 (JG).
[41] MDC-T activists, Matobo, 10 November 2013 (JG).

The MDC did not look like a party that could take power. Even its supporters said it was 'in chaos', 'like a crippled child'.[42]

Voters who had been keenly supportive in the past lost heart:

> I didn't vote, I didn't even register. I thought there was no choice. The MDC has performed so badly.[43]

The lack of organisational capacity led many supporters to question the good faith of its leaders. For others it highlighted the party's naivety. This was no less devastating as it demonstrated the party's weak understanding of the political process. They failed to realise what ZANU-PF was up to, they did not grasp the importance of organising their supporters, and they misunderstood the way electoral politics works in Zimbabwe. For one MDC stalwart, it was a question of MDC innocence in the face of ZANU-PF corruption, backed up by regional interference:

> [T]he MDC underestimated the manipulations that the
> government was prepared for ... The MDC overly trusted
> the process in places as if everyone was hoping to see things
> getting back to normal which ZANU was not prepared [to let
> happen] ... The MDC was mad to see that the African guys
> [SADC and AU] were going to oversee a free and fair
> election.[44]

For a CSO activist in Bulawayo, the party's arrogance led them to ignore the warning signs:

> The opposition went into the election unprepared. They did not
> have the voters' list. Civil society kept on raising that issue, but the
> attendance when people were campaigning, you had thousands of
> MDC, they were saying even if they rig we will wing it. They then

---

[42] MDC-N activist, Bulawayo, 9 November 2013; MDC-T activist, Chitungwiza, 3 November 2013 (JG).

[43] Businessman, Bulawayo, 9 November 2013 (JG).

[44] MDC activist, Chitungwiza, 3 November 2013 (JG).

> relaxed. They were preparing for power. People kept saying, what is your plan B? There was no need. That became a problem.[45]

Some blamed Tsvangirai for a lack of oversight over a lazy or ineffective team:

> Morgan's team was out of touch, thought they were too smart to keep in touch with the grass roots. His team is entirely responsible for the election strategy. Morgan assumed that all his people were working with zeal and passion and they were not.[46]

And one MDC candidate admitted to a failure of strategy:

> We were all duped. I was clueless. We all have to take responsibility for the strategic weaknesses.[47]

However, most devastating of all were the MDC parties' failures to come up with policies that resonated with voters. The MDCs' connections to the West, their lack of clarity on land (underlined by support from the country's white farmers) and their abstract policies instead created an uneasy sense of dissonance with voters. This was backed up by fears that the parties lacked wealth and the power to assume effective control of the country.

Both MDC parties were criticised for their policies. The MDC-T spoke the language of democracy and human rights, while the MDC-N promised devolution to its largely Ndebele constituency. Although both parties continually addressed issues of jobs and housing, these were not the issues that people associated with them. In 2013, human rights and devolution lost out to material issues such as land, food and jobs.

> The MDC is from the people by the people. It is supported by everybody here. It is a democratic party and everybody

---

[45] CSO leader, Bulawayo, 8 November 2013 (JG).
[46] Trade unionist, Harare, 5 November 2013 (JG).
[47] MDC candidate, Bulawayo, 7 November 2013 (JG).

needs democracy. They need democracy, but first they need food on their table.[48]

I asked a man why did you vote for ZANU-PF? He said: they brought food, community share ownership – this for them is development. The MDC talks devolution.[49]

ZANU-PF has delivered real change and improvement to people's lives and that's true. The MDC dismissed the empowerment and indigenisation programme. The 10 per cent delivers schools and clinics and roads. It's ZANU-PF that is doing that and the MDC is talking about human rights and respect for the law. That's academic: it doesn't put bread on the table.[50]

This lack of resonance was perceived as a terrible failure of sympathy between the opposition parties and the electorate.

I think both MDCs don't understand their own voters. If their voters ask for sadza, they bring tea. ZANU knows that people want farms.[51]

When discussing this lack of sympathy, people often pointed to the MDC parties' close connections to Western backers and white farmers: as a result, they had become too Western in their style and priorities. This problem was explored in the discussion between MDC activists in Bulawayo:

Our guys speak fluent English. They read too many of your books and it doesn't appeal to a person in a rural area.

These politicians read too many English books. What people want is not what the books say. If my kids are not well, I expect the MP to take them to hospital.

But if he raised the issue of hyenas attacking people in our areas, then they will say, here is a man who understands us.

---

[48] Political activist, Matabeleland South, 10 November 2013 (JG).
[49] MDC-N activist, Bulawayo, 9 November 2013 (JG).
[50] CSO leader, Harare, 4 November 2013 (JG).
[51] Sadza, a maize porridge, is Zimbabwe's national dish. MDC activist, Bulawayo, 9 November 2013 (JG).

> We tend to dwell too much on the urban population and not
> enough on the rural. And the numbers are larger in the rural area.
> I come from Lupane. I have never seen a minister. The MDC was
> busy with the urban population, copying Obama, using facebook.
> But most people [in the rural areas] don't use facebook.[52]

Other problems for the MDC were its inability to state clearly that it
would not return farms to their former white owners. People who had
been given farms feared that they would be taken back if the MDC
won, and others who hoped to benefit from redistribution also assumed
they would do better under ZANU-PF. Added to that, the MDC-T's
equivocation on the issue of homosexuality raised concerns was cited
as another example of the Western – and therefore un-Zimbabwean –
influence. These problems were cited across the country:

> He was not clear on the land question or on homosexuality. The
> Christian community think Tsvangirai can tolerate satanism and
> homosexuality. ZANU capitalised on that. It is very important. If a
> president says yes yes to homosexuality that frightens a lot of
> people. The connection with the West destroyed Tsvangirai.[53]

Activists in Bulawayo told a similar story:

> Most white people support gays. So Morgan had to say he likes gays.
>   We were funded by white farmers so we had to run away from
> that issue. The pictures of those white farmers signing cheques was
> the downfall of the MDC.[54]

Another tangible factor that held many people back from voting for
the MDC parties was their lack of financial and political clout. The
parties might once have been excused their poverty, but having been
in government, they should have built up wealth reserves that could
be used to express their substance and capacity to run the country.

---

[52] MDC-N activists, Bulawayo, 9 November 2013 (JG).

[53] CSO leader, Harare, 4 November 2013 (JG).

[54] MDC-N activist, Bulawayo, 9 November 2013 (JG).

This lack seemed to be exemplified in the poorly funded election campaign, and it underlined the parties' lack of capacity. This was felt particularly acutely in Matabeleland, a region where people feel they have been systematically deprived of resources ever since independence in 1980. Here, the MDC's apparent poverty was a sign of its lack of leadership capacity. The following comments are all from political and civil society activists in Matabeleland:

> They have no money – the MDC campaigns are not funded. MPs get about 200 t-shirts if they are lucky, 500 posters and $300 ... The MDC candidates walk. People ... think that you have nothing and will steal.[55]
>
> If these guys had given people money they would be in power now. So it's their own fault ... In 2000 when the party was formed, it was poor but the little they had would come to the people. Now they say they don't have money, they're not in government. So people will see that nothing is coming their way. These MDC guys went to government and came out poor.[56]
>
> The MDC manifesto said it would create jobs. People bought that. But they didn't bring things. They were saying they would create jobs but they could only do that if they won. ZANU-PF gave food now. People who are not politically mature want food now ... Between human rights and money, people will choose money.[57]
>
> When the MDCs win seats they don't have power, they can't produce anything for the people. ZANU controls everything.[58]

All this goes to underline the most extraordinary outcome of the 2013 elections: the opposition parties' failures in Matabeleland. It was encapsulated by a teacher who lives in Old Pumula, a township outside Bulawayo:

[55] CSO leader, Bulawayo, 8 November 2013 (JG).
[56] MDC-T activist, Matobo, 10 November 2013 (JG).
[57] Political activist, Matobo, 10 November 2013 (JG).
[58] MDC-N activists, Bulawayo, 9 November 2013 (JG).

> Why is it that these people who are still reeling under the consequences of Gukurahundi would vote for ZANU-PF? Either it was high voter apathy, or people simply said no, we are tired of supporting a loser.[59]

Three months after the elections, activists assembled a picture of an MDC in a terrible state. Its party structures were in bad repair, battered by in-fighting and a lack of discipline that spilled out in public. Its supporters felt that the party's once strong networks and unifying spirit – forged in the difficult days of opposition – had melted away as elites had begun to taste the pleasures of office. They appeared to have pulled the ladders up after themselves, leaving their grass roots without moral or material support. This left activists unable or disinclined to attempt to woo voters who had begun to question the party's abilities, either to perform in government or to represent their interests. None of this appeared to have been recognised by the party, which ran a badly organised and lacklustre campaign, apparently complacent that the electorate would be steadfast in its support. This litany of disaster spilled over into virtually every discussion of MDC activists. Their party had bungled the election. How did ZANU-PF win it? This is the question we address in the next chapter.

[59] Teacher, Old Pumula, 9 November 2013 (JG).

5 'ZANU Managed to Mend Relationships'

The ZANU-PF Campaign

Many Zimbabweans worried that ZANU-PF might try to steal the election by rigging it. During the election campaign itself there were rumours about Nikuv, the Israeli company the party was supposed to have hired to help them run their campaign. The company was said to be well versed in electoral manipulation, and even before polling day there were many stories about the way special voting for members of the security forces had been stacked: soldiers and police officers were lined up to vote in order, so their choices could be traced afterwards, or commanding officers stood over them while they voted.

A huge election monitoring exercise was mounted by the civil society organisation ZESN – the Zimbabwe Election Support Network. Thousands of volunteers from church, union and civil society organisations attended training days so that they could be posted to polling stations around the country. One session was held in a school on the outskirts of Harare.[1] Forty men and women from Mashonaland, Masvingo and Harare were given a crash course on the basics of the new constitution and the electoral process. Sitting in classroom rows, they carefully took notes as they were told how the polling stations are laid out, how far the policeman should stand outside the door, how many election officials should be there, what equipment each should have, from ballot papers to indelible ink and the official stamp, what time the polling station should open, what time it should close, who could help voters needing assistance and in what ways, what constituted a spoiled ballot paper, and where the results were to be posted once the count was finished. They were given forms to fill in details about the number of electors who were

---

[1] Gallagher attended this event and took part in the training activities.

turned away and counts of ballot papers used, as well as 'serious incident forms' to file in case they witnessed transgressions of the process. They were given careful instructions on their personal safety ('we want living heroes, not dead heroes'), on how to deal with SADC observers (polite, but not too friendly), and what to do if things weren't quite right ('it is your job to point out problems, leave the arguing to the party monitors').

These people – ordinary citizens – were there to keep the process straight, 'and we know this will be difficult, because this is Africa, this is Zimbabwe', said the instructor. Most were convinced that the ruling party would try to rig the election, and they saw their job being to keep it free and fair, and to record the voting process so that ZESN could produce an authoritative account afterwards.

At the end of the day they stood, raised their right hands and together read out the election observers' charter. They would not display party symbols or campaign for any party; they would not interfere in the election process; they would commit themselves to the constitution, the authority of the Zimbabwe Electoral Commission.

There were many stories of rigging from election observers and party agents. People told about busloads of voters arriving from out of town carrying registration slips but no ID; others of people turned away because their names were not on the register, or of people who were 'assisted' in voting by party officials or police officers. There were stories about the indelible ink that is used to mark voters' fingers to stop multiple voting – apparently it washed off easily – of disappearing ink used to mark the ballot papers themselves. The most incredible of these included the ink that was used to make a cross next to an MDC candidate's name then faded off and reappeared in the ZANU-PF box. There were stories of voters being paid or fed chicken and chips; of some election officials falling asleep and others hiding ballot papers. Several people talked about polling stations that the opposition parties only found out about towards the end of polling day.

Many of these stories were aired at a conference for CSOs held in one of Harare's grand hotels three months after the election.[2] Representatives from across the country gathered to talk through the shocking result – most were MDC members or sympathisers – and heartbreaking stories were told about a stolen election. There was only one discourse on offer here. Nobody discussed the failures of MDC parties. And neither did any of them begin to venture into a discussion of whether the ZANU-PF victory might be down to factors other than cheating. Cheating, it was clear, there was. But was it decisive? The question was not raised.

Only afterwards, over a quiet drink by the hotel's swimming pool, did the issue come up. A CSO representative from Matabeleland said: 'ZANU-PF won the election. There was rigging, yes, but it wasn't significant.'[3]

This chapter explores how ZANU-PF did it. Drawing on the accounts of activists from all parties who witnessed the campaign on the ground, it details a professional and committed campaign that had involved a substantial voter registration drive, effective party mobilisation and a carefully crafted re-seduction of the Zimbabwean electorate. While the MDC had been focused on the GNU, and assuming that they just had to 'finish ZANU-PF off',[4] ZANU-PF had been organising and executing a brilliantly planned five-year election campaign. As one ZANU-PF activist explained:

> Immediately after 2008 they never stopped campaigning. They went to all rural areas and urban places to campaign. They were able to capitalise on the weaknesses of those [MDC] people put into ministries. They worked very hard. From 2008 they never left the people.[5]

---

[2] Gallagher attended this conference.
[3] CSO activist, Harare, 13 November 2013 (JG).
[4] CSO activist, Bulawayo, 11 November 2013 (JG).
[5] ZANU-PF activists, Bulawayo, 11 November 2013 (JG).

MDC-sympathisers around the country reluctantly agreed:

> ZANU-PF was very thorough. Theirs was a military operation. They were stage-managing this for the international and regional audiences ... ZANU-PF did not leave any stone unturned. They ensured supporters were assisted. They did not take things for granted.[6]

Although opposition activists continued to complain about uneven playing fields – the bulk of the resources, the state-controlled media, and the security forces were all largely on the ruling party's side – and about coercion and election rigging, many admitted that they had also been outclassed. Somehow, ZANU-PF had managed to reconnect with the electorate in ways they had failed to do for years. A civil society leader based in Bulawayo said:

> I attended one of Robert Mugabe's rallies. I drove by. There were people who were bused [in], but, there is a road from the western areas where people would walk to White City, and from there, they were flocking.[7]

In discussions with political activists three months after the elections, three key ZANU-PF strengths emerged; it is these with which this chapter is concerned. They are clustered around the issues of materialism, fear and leadership. The importance of the material was clearly understood by ZANU-PF, and in this they showed a much sharper sense of the electorate than did the MDC, as detailed in the last chapter. Fear – the residual effects of the violence of 2008 – was an important, if hidden factor, particularly in ZANU-PF's rural heartlands and in the poorest urban areas. And finally the issue of leadership, by which we mean both the leadership of Mugabe himself, and the authority he and his party were able to establish through their ability to embody a wider sense of Zimbabweanness,

---

[6] CSO activist, Bulawayo, 11 November 2013 (JG).
[7] CSO activist, Bulawayo, 8 November 2013 (JG).

were crucial in pulling voters back to what was successfully portrayed as the 'party of independence'.

MATERIALISM

> We have this very materialist approach to voting ... The opposition offers nothing tangible.[8]

This comment was made, in the dark, in the suburban offices of a CSO in Bulawayo. The interview with the head of the organisation had begun in the late afternoon, and the discussion gradually moved on from the election itself and onto Zimbabwe's political culture. As evening approached and other workers left for home we continued to talk into the dark – the electricity failed, as it often does – and the mosquitoes got quietly to work.

The head of this CSO, who has been a vocal supporter of the MDC in the past, explained how even in Matabeleland voters were effectively wooed by ZANU-PF's ability to represent material success. It was an analysis that we found everywhere, like the material itself – the presents made by ZANU PF of party caps and maize, and in promises of things to come, from farms to share ownership. He said:

> We saw a shift in our social politics. The labour movement was destroyed by unemployment. ZANU-PF managed to respond to the informal sector fast. Farmers got land, miners got security. They identified and supported cross-border traders. The patronage approach really worked for ZANU-PF to give them numbers ... When people say they are voting for a government, it is for someone who can give them everything. They are not ready to look after themselves. [Particularly] in the rural areas, leadership works along this pattern.[9]

Activists from all parties agreed that the tangible things the parties offered were of enormous significance to the effectiveness of their campaigns. As two MDC activists described:

---

[8] CSO activist, Bulawayo, 11 November 2013 (JG).   [9] Ibid.

> ZANU-PF would go house by house giving 2kg of rice, some pots.
> That link might help with votes ... Mugabe went everywhere – he
> was the most serious candidate, he was the most visible.
>
> During election time it was a free-for-all. Politicians gave out rice
> and promised them areas to build their houses. The appeal of
> ZANU was direct and immediate.[10]

The effects of this were several. In the first place, ZANU-PF's gifts
represented something solid – rice, pots, t-shirts are things that people
need. Many people who are very poor valued these gifts. Further, the
gifts represented an important symbolic marker of respect, signalling
that the party took its supporters seriously. And finally, they offered
an indication of a more general approach to the business of governing,
one where the ruling party's job is to provide material things directly
to people. As one village headman said:

> ZANU-PF was giving everyone caps, t-shirts, Zambias and
> bandanas and the opposition was giving to party members [only].
> I was angry that I didn't get anything. The MDC didn't give to
> all the people, they didn't recognise all the people. People were
> complaining ... I realise people have been in this party for 13 years
> and they have nothing to show for it. If you join ZANU-PF you
> will become rich today.[11]

The abundance in particular of ZANU-PF regalia created a strong
impression of party strength. Although many people pointed out that
the caps and t-shirts were often worn as a 'fashion statement' rather
than as a sign of political allegiance, their ubiquity had an important
psychological effect. One civil society activist said:

> Food and t-shirts made a difference. Ten years ago you would
> not see a youth wearing a ZANU-PF t-shirt and cap – now

---

[10] MDC-N activists, Bulawayo, 9 November 2013 (JG).
[11] A Zambia is a piece of cloth women wear over their skirts. Village headman,
Matabeleland South, 10 November 2013 (JG).

it is usual. That has an impact – it gives people the impression that ZANU-PF has people.[12]

And another pointed out: 'If there is a sea of green t-shirts, you begin to feel isolated.'[13]

ZANU-PF's gift-giving created a powerful and direct impression of connection with voters, of universal coverage, and of an understanding of the needs of the people. This impression underpinned the party's broader policy approach, and the sense of its capacity – also crucial aspects of the effectiveness of the campaign.

On policy, the party created a campaign that spoke directly to the immediate material needs of the population. Brian Raftopoulos has described how ZANU-PF has managed to create new forms of 'governmentality' through the distribution of land and of informal trade and mining privileges, effectively embedding itself as an essential element in the livelihoods of many thousands of Zimbabweans (Raftopoulos, 2013: 980). This appeals to 'entrepreneurial dynamism', but also carries an implicit threat that with the end of ZANU-PF, the fragile economic framework, which many have managed to grasp hold of, will crumble and leave them without resources.

Building on its record of land reform – in which many small-scale farmers were given land and have begun to establish a more secure living for themselves – the party's Indigenisation Programme promised community share ownership of mines and private enterprise. The party's promises, and record of delivery on them, were one of its most effective campaign tools. One ZANU-PF activist thought that land was the key to the election: 'Zimbabweans are very excited at having their pieces of land. That is what made them [ZANU-PF] win the hearts of people.'[14] Many activists who are critical of the ruling party argue that the schemes undermine the wider economy, dampening agricultural exports and frightening away

[12] CSO leader, Bulawayo, 8 November 2013 (JG).
[13] CSO activist, Bulawayo, 11 November 2013 (JG).
[14] ZANU-PF activist, Bulawayo, 11 November 2013 (JG).

potential foreign investors. Yet they also acknowledge the real benefits the schemes bring to many individuals. One head of an NGO that
works with farmers in Mashonaland Central said:

> From the small farmer's perspective, there has been an
> improvement. If you look at the assets people have been able to
> acquire ... I know friends who owned six, seven, eight tonne trucks.
> They would go and collect crops to take to market, but they are no
> longer profitable. A lot of farmers have bought their own small
> trucks so they can take their own and their neighbours' crops ...
> [ZANU-PF's] policies are trying to bring popular policies to support
> the farmer even if economically it may make no sense. At the short-
> term level, that will strengthen the position of ZANU-PF on the
> ground.[15]

Alongside the small-scale farmers and informal workers, some
members of the middle class also flourished during the GNU period.
Existing and aspiring middle classes now saw the potential benefits
of an affiliation with ZANU-PF. One Harare-based businessman
who I (JG) met over breakfast in a guesthouse on the outskirts of
Bulawayo, explained how the political landscape had shifted for him
and his family.

> The problem for the MDC is that the middle class grew very well
> under the GNU. My brother did very well – he bought two houses.
> When he has a party for his kid in grade 7 he invites 500 people. He
> used to be a strong MDC man. Now he is ZANU-PF. He sees many
> opportunities from the Indigenisation Programme and being part of
> ZANU. These middle-class people are very influential.[16]

Opposition activists were in confusion as to the benefits and draw-
backs of these resource reallocations. Some believed that ZANU-PF
had created a scramble for resources which sucked individuals into a

---

[15] NGO head, Mashonaland Central, 14 November 2013 (JG).
[16] Businessman, Harare, interviewed in Bulawayo, 9 November 2013 (JG).

race for patronage and the resources that came with it. For them this was a giant con and they refused to acknowledge that significant economic shifts were underway:

> After the farm and company grabs people who had been left out see that others have benefitted – now I can benefit. No one in the MDC has benefitted so I need to join ZANU-PF ... People are fooled to think I am going to be rich.[17]

These MDC loyalists pointed out that the promise of material gain was an illusion, or would be bought at the expense of long-term economic growth. Land reform had already cut Zimbabwe's agricultural production dramatically; now the forced indigenisation of private companies would kill off the country's moribund private sector by scaring off investors.

But others saw the changes as substantial. Some of them had to admit that the policies were gradually amounting to a real redistribution of resources. Poor people were not foolishly chasing the dream of wealth: they were voting for policies that really had the power to change their lives. One pro-MDC civil society activist said:

> The real story is about how ZANU-PF met the needs of people. They resettled farmers and they allowed prospectors to pan for gold freely and lots came. It became clear that these farmers many of them were making a good living. They didn't want to lose that. In parts of Matobo the Shared Ownership Scheme is really working for people. They have schools and clinics. They are becoming better off. These are not token changes, they are real.[18]

The opposition parties' failure of imagination meant that it could not or would not be drawn into the same game. The MDC, equivocal on land, was successfully portrayed as a threat to these burgeoning livelihoods.

---

[17] MDC-T activist, Chitungwiza, 3 November 2013 (JG).
[18] Civil society activist, Bulawayo, interviewed in Harare, 13 November 2013 (JG).

> ZANU-PF has got land, money, projects in their wards so they
> were saying, if you vote for the MDC they will take all this back.
> Three quarters of the community would believe that the MDC
> would give land back to the whites.[19]

Crucially for ZANU-PF success, the party appeared to carry the
wherewithal to deliver on its programme. Election promises do not
amount to much without the capacity and power to make them
happen. Here again ZANU-PF was dramatically ahead of the
opposition parties. The party demonstrably had the resources and
the clout to make an effective government. This was apparent during
the campaign itself, as Tendi has described, 'Mugabe's campaign was
slick, well-funded, united and peaceful' (2013: 963).

A group of rural voters described how the well-resourced
ZANU-PF team created a good impression of the party's organisational and financial capacity. Motobo is in the national park where
Cecil Rhodes is buried, an area of stunning beauty, and once the
destination for thousands of tourists every year. This community used
to make a good living selling carvings to visitors, but since the economic decline and political instability, this livelihood has dried up.
Sitting in an open hut in the middle of the homestead of the village
headman, several of them worked on delicately carved boxes
decorated with animal heads as they spoke. They explained how
ZANU-PF's appeal rested on its promise of connectivity – to the rest
of the country, and to state power and resources. For this group,
ZANU-PF appeared able and willing to bridge the gap between their
community and the state, a gap that was experienced both geographic-
ally and in terms of access to the attributes of modernity:

> Every MP had a car. Even Mugabe was like a general who was able
> to bring the party together and the whole country.
>
> There's no difference between ZANU-PF and the government –
> they hold all the resources.

---

[19] MDC-T activist, Matabeleland South, 10 November 2013 (JG).

We have no problem with where he gets the money from [the State] as long as he brings money to the people.[20]

Their feeling of being forgotten led them to reassess the potential of a ZANU-PF government that had the capacity to change their lives, and now appeared to be prepared to take them seriously.

The importance of capacity was explained further by a group of MDC activists.

> The whole issue is about the reality on the ground. What we are looking at is how the people, in their long journey, are looking for immediate solutions. The one who can carry that out is the one in power, the one with money. That is only ZANU-PF. ZANU is everywhere. For immediate solutions for people from any corner of Zimbabwe [they] would have to approach ZANU-PF.
>
> In Bindura, this ZANU guy was saying, I will sort out your roads. He gets on his phone and the caterpillars arrived during the meeting. He would say, you're hungry, he would phone and the tractors with maize would come.[21]

This powerful image was constantly compared to the poverty of the opposition parties, the 'guys who went into government and came out poor'. ZANU-PF capitalised on the opposition's cautious approach to spending, and this was noticed. One voter in rural Matabeleland said: 'ZANU-PF people are saying these guys are saying their hands are tied up and they can't do anything for you. So if they can't untie their hands, then vote for us.'[22] And the CSO leader, speaking in his dark Bulawayo office put it like this:

> ZANU-PF creates a narrative that describes no ZANU-PF without Mugabe, and no Zimbabwe without ZANU-PF. They have patronage, so everyone must seem to be buying it and showing they believe in it. The culture of bootlicking. 'I am ZANU-PF so I have

---

[20] Rural voters, Matabeleland South 10 November 2013 (JG).
[21] MDC-N activists, Bulawayo 9 November 2013 (JG).
[22] Rural voter, Matabeleland South 10 November 2013 (JG).

authority and people listen and fear me. We are in power, being in charge, better than others.' It always comes back to the material.[23]

Material issues affected voters up and down the country, the poor and the middle classes. However, although voters in Harare and Chitung-wiza did talk about share ownership, and gifts were an issue for people living in ZANU-PF rural strongholds, these things were of particular importance in Matabeleland. The result in Matabeleland was one of the most startling aspects of the 2013 elections, described by one observer as 'a shocker'.[24] The region which has suffered repression and years of marginalisation since independence has always been staunchly anti-ZANU-PF. And yet here, where people usually open their accounts of the history of the country with references to the suffering they experienced in the Gukurahundi campaign in the 1980s, and where many people argue that their region is being colonised by the Shona, ZANU-PF won all but the two Bulawayo parliamentary seats.

Activists accounted for this by pointing out that people in Matabeleland were fed up of deprivation. The opposition parties they have supported over the years have failed to make any difference to the region. In particular, five years of the GNU – which to many in Matabeleland, where the party swept the board in 2008, appeared to be the MDC in power – was another failure. One possible explanation for the ZANU-PF victory in Matabeleland is that voters, exhausted by poverty and marginalisation, now felt they could do nothing but join the national party. The region threw in the towel.

FEAR AND VIOLENCE

The 2013 elections were the most peaceful for years. All contenders made a point of condemning violence and asking for a calm political contest, and they achieved one. The election even had its moments of humour, as in the witty use by both parties of a photograph of

---

[23] Civil society activist, Bulawayo, 11 November 2013 (JG).
[24] European diplomat, Harare 6 November 2013 (JG).

Tsvangirai and other MDC leaders reading the ZANU-PF manifesto.[25] But this is not to suggest that fear was not a weapon in this election. Violence, although not overt, was in the back of many people's minds throughout. This was particularly the case in the ZANU-PF strongholds in Mashonaland and the Midlands where one could hear plenty of stories of the violence of 2008, and in poor urban areas where people are continuously intimidated and threatened by ZANU-PF's youth militia.

There are a number of elements to this. One relates to the implicit threat of violence carried in memories of 2008, which caused many people to at least hide their political affiliation. As one NGO worker who lives in Mashonaland Central explained:

> In the rural areas especially in the former commercial farms, anything associated with the MDC will land you in trouble – even talking [about the party] is promoting [it] and saying that you want our land repossessed ... MDC supporters were given t-shirts but they could not put them on. I had one but didn't wear it. They were saying, we want peace, but people thought they could be lying to us – people remembered 2008.[26]

And a head teacher from the same region said:

> This [election] was very peaceful. People were very relieved. But it was peaceful in the sense that people had memories of the last one, so they would go for ZANU-PF [because] they would have memories of the punishment they perceived they would be getting [if they didn't] ... In 2000 it was about 70 per cent in favour of the MDC. In 2007 things began to change when there was a lot of

[25] ZANU-PF ran a newspaper advertisement with a photograph of Tsvangirai, Finance Minister Tendai Biti and other MDC-T officials reading a copy of the ZANU-PF manifesto. The caption ran: 'Our manifesto has excited everyone!' The following day, the MDC-T came right back at them, showing the same picture but with speech bubbles. Biti says: 'ZANU yazopererwa manje [ZANU is finished now]' while Tsvangirai replies: 'Haiwawo! Musapedzere nguva nenyaya dzanezuro! [Don't waste your time with these old lies!]'.

[26] NGO worker, Mashonaland Central, 14 November 2013 (JG).

intimidation. It became a 50/50 situation. Then 2008 to now, it's in favour of ZANU-PF because of that fear. If you would try to assemble people to a ZANU-PF rally, they would go because they know the consequences of not going. But for an MDC rally, they don't go because they are frightened.[27]

A civil society activist who works in Harare's slum areas said:

The threat was in the minds of people. ZANU-PF youths in hushed tones had implied that if you vote for the MDC we are going to repeat the 2008 drama. They didn't need to deploy their violence machinery.[28]

One civil society activist in Mashonaland believed that this internal-ised fear was vital in securing a ZANU-PF victory, and he also used it to explain the high number of assisted votes:

What they did in 2008 was intentional and it's still very clear in people's minds. They made it very peaceful [this time] but people feared the violence would come back ... people were aware that if they voted MDC they might get back to 2008. A lot of people who said they can't write said that because they wanted people to see they had voted correctly [for ZANU-PF].[29]

People not only feared reprisals for voting 'incorrectly': many worried that their tenuous hold on a living would be threatened by a change to the status quo. Violence has slipped into the way many of the most vulnerable people conduct their livelihoods. The ability of the urban poor to access trading stands in markets, to obtain trading permits and to avoid police harassment is intimately wound up with their political affiliation. In some areas, having ZANU-PF connections is essential to keeping your family alive, and anything that jeopardises that is to be avoided. Harare's Mbare, scene of the brutal Murambatsvina campaign where houses were bulldozed by the police in 2005, is one such area.

---

[27] Head teacher, Mashonaland Central, 14 November 2013 (JG).
[28] CSO leader, Harare, 4 November (JG).
[29] NGO head, Mashonaland Central, 14 November 2013 (JG).

Everywhere in Mbare there are vendors. They were allowed there by ZANU-PF who said they must be allowed to make a living. ZANU has created the conditions for destitution and desperation and given them the protection of the law ... They are acting like a saviour. The poor people, very ignorant people, these people believe in ZANU-PF ... They have problems but they cannot go against ZANU-PF. ZANU protects them. They need police protection. In them there is no hope for a better life than this ... They are supporting the government because it offers them a way to support themselves, a way of making a living. If they support the MDC they are victimised and evicted.[30]

The fear of losing livelihoods extends into the issue of land which is still controlled by the largely ZANU-PF loyal village headmen. The MDC came to be seen as a threat, as one group of activists who tried to campaign in a ZANU-PF rural area discovered:

The ZANU-PF message meant people were voting for ZANU to keep their farms. We were once nearly attacked as MDC activists by the community. The language that their leadership was using was that if the MDC would win, you will lose your farms. The traditional leaders said this.[31]

For the opposition it is frustrating to see how the ZANU-PF logic has seeped into people's sense of their ability to survive. 'ZANU-PF creates a situation and then comes in as a saviour,' explained one MDC activist, while another said: 'This is a party that has survived by keeping people poor and insecure.'[32] One man likened this to an abusive relationship.

People are not employed. If you come as a saviour they love you. The government is like a demagogue, people are very emotional

---

[30] CSO leader, Harare, 4 November (JG).

[31] MDC-N activist, Bulawayo 9 November 2013 (JG).

[32] MDC-T activist, Chitungwiza, 3 November; Trade union activist, Harare 5 November 2013 (JG).

about that. You make them suffer and then you come with promises and people will believe you. They torture you and then offer to help you. Now people are thinking about their stomachs. Even me, if I was offered $1,000 I would say that is what I want.[33]

Also damaging for the opposition parties was the perception that an MDC victory would have unleashed a violent backlash by the security forces, possibly a civil war. This point was made several times during interviews.

What I have observed is that God came on the side of Zimbabweans because if Tsvangirai had won I would say by now the situation would be like in Mozambique – thousands would have been killed, thousands would have fled and Tsvangirai would not have been seated in State House because of the violent resistance to him by the security services and the police.[34]

Slowly but surely people are starting to prioritise the issue of political stability. If they make the opposition win, there is likely to be war in this country. People chose peace, not violence ... Since independence, ZANU has been winning elections. In 2002 people had hoped ZANU was going down the drain. In 2008 from what we saw, the MDC won, and they were rigged. This time I think people got tired and said, this guy is not prepared to relinquish power.[35]

Because of this, a peaceful election meant a widespread submission to a ZANU-PF victory. Violence, hiding behind the scenes, was a powerful tool for ZANU-PF, intimidating voters and creating a logic that made MDC success a dangerous prospect. This was overwhelmingly the case in ZANU-PF strongholds and amongst the country's poorest where fear has created an atmosphere of deep anxiety and effectively shut down their ability and possibly even their desire to try to bring about change.

[33] Teacher, township near Bulawayo, 9 November 2013 (JG).
[34] Civil society leader, Harare, 4 November 2013 (JG).
[35] Teacher, township near Bulawayo, 9 November 2013 (JG).

Research for this book suggests that violence had less of an effect in Matabeleland. There, people claim to have become immune to intimidation, having experienced violence for much longer. They are often prepared to talk much more freely about their political views and to dismiss the need for anonymity. But amongst the most vulnerable people in the urban areas, and amongst the ZANU-PF heartlands in Mashonaland in particular, violence appears to have been internalised to such a degree that its overt use is no longer necessary. It is much more difficult to conduct research here. Most people present an opaque or anodyne account of political developments. Those that do talk frankly insist on meeting in secret. Several interviewees said that if their names were used they would be killed.

Despite their apparent peacefulness and even cheerful character, the 2013 elections were propelled by a powerful undercurrent of fear. Members of a group of MDC activists who live in Chitungwiza put it most strongly: 'It was exactly the same as 2008. The difference is they didn't do it publicly. They will do the bad evil quietly.'[36]

LEADERSHIP

Over our breakfast in a Bulawayo guesthouse, a businessman from Harare explained how he lost faith in the MDC by comparing the leadership capacities of Tsvangirai and Mugabe. For him, and for many Zimbabweans, the idea of Mugabe as leader, and his clearly apparent qualities, make it difficult to accept what many see as an inferior replacement.

> I think when it came down to it, people do still respect Mugabe. They want him to be what he was. He is very impressive – his intellect, the way he touches people. I think people want him to be their liberation leader again.[37]

Robert Mugabe has been the master of Zimbabwean politics for the whole of the country's life. People have powerful feelings about the

---

[36] MDC activists, Chitungwiza, 3 November 2013 (JG).
[37] Businessman, Harare, interviewed in Bulawayo, 9 November 2013 (JG).

man who led them to independence and who went on to unleash violent campaigns against many of them. It is not difficult to find people who are prepared to express extremely negative feelings about him. In the years of the GNU, I (JG) have heard Mugabe described as 'power-hungry', 'cheap and childish', 'dishonest', a man who 'hates good things'.[38] One woman asked: 'Can they not do what they did to Saddam Hussein? I would like to see Mugabe hiding in a hole in the ground.'[39] But alongside the scorn, there are feelings of attachment and respect for Mugabe's political skills and intelligence. Mugabe has variously been described as 'a genius', 'British at heart ... a man of his word' and 'very impressive ... [able to] touch people'.[40] Several times people have said that Mugabe could have been better than Mandela, if only he had not been corrupted by so long in office.

Tendi has described how Mugabe was able to demonstrate his powerful political skills during the election campaign in 2013, decisively making a last-minute appeal to voters in a television address on the eve of the polls (2013). And these skills are widely recognised. During the campaign, when many were predicting that the president would lose the election, people spoke almost regretfully about his political demise. 'Every politician is held up to Robert Mugabe. Mugabe listens very well, very critically, and he can make appropriate responses.'[41] Tsvangirai, as we saw in the last chapter, could not match Mugabe's authority:

> He still has it. The guy is powerful. He has the president's office, the CIO, the state security – those guys are 100 per cent loyal to him ... Every politician is held up to Robert Mugabe.[42]

---

[38] Mbare resident, 2 September 2011; civil society worker, 2 September 2011; Old Pumula resident, 30 May 2012; Mbare resident, 1 September 2011 (JG).

[39] Chitungwiza resident, 4 September 2011 (JG).

[40] NGO worker, Mashonaland Central, 14 November 2013; Civil society leader, Harare, 4 November 2013; Businessman, Harare, interviewed in Bulawayo, 9 November 2013 (JG).

[41] CSO leader, Harare, 4 November 2013 (JG).

[42] Civil society leader, Harare, 4 November 2013 (JG).

This intense and ambivalent relationship both with Mugabe and ZANU-PF itself played an important role in the 2013 elections. Underlying the rage and despair at what had happened to the country lurks a residual and powerful connection to the ruling party. ZANU-PF was able to stir this up during its campaign, and to reconnect with voters in a way that saw many expressing almost a sense of relief and homecoming. They did this both through their policies, and in the ways they went out to the people.

The party's policies and priorities resonated with voters in a way that the MDC completely missed. These include the issues of race and land that were embodied for many in the liberation struggle. One white MDC candidate said:

> They are a liberation party who get stirred up by talk about war. It doesn't resonate amongst the people I mix with. Land and race have been created as a propaganda tool. The media gives out a message to the world. They don't represent the people anywhere. I didn't see any celebrations. The land and race thing is just a classical myth.[43]

But he was the only one. All the others – including MDC supporters – disagreed. One trade union activist, who speaks from the perspective of the organisation that Tsvangirai used to lead, and which gave birth to the MDC, admitted the continuing power of the race issue. She said:

> There are racial issues. There is skewed distribution of wealth . . . the racial divide is still very strong. You see it in industry. All the directors are whites, but not the front-line staff. This is why the indigenisation and empowerment programme has resonance, even if it's a very stupid programme.[44]

Race, land and liberation are impossible to separate, and they are issues that Mugabe has made his own.

---

[43] MDC politician, Bulawayo, 7 November 2013 (JG).
[44] Trade union activist, Harare 5 November 2013 (JG).

> The land issue is very important to Zimbabweans. We all want to be farmers ... All the big guys have farms. Mugabe's rhetoric on land and race really resonated with Zimbabweans. It means a lot to them.[45]
>
> You would be surprised at the numbers that go to see the liberation fighters being buried. There is still an emotional attachment to the liberation struggle ... Look at the number of people who lost brothers and children, who don't know where their mothers or fathers are. It's difficult to remove that emotional attachment. Whoever wants to be a leader must show appreciation for what happened in the liberation struggle.[46]

Particularly for older Zimbabweans, Mugabe's nationalist message still resonates. Tsvangirai, who was not part of the struggle, and who is seen to depend on the support of white farmers and the West, could not tap into this feeling. Indeed, as we saw in the previous chapter, his association with the West came to be seen in 2013 as compromising his ability to represent and embody Zimbabwe. Mugabe has no such difficulty, and has made the most of his credentials as a freedom fighter and anti-colonialist.

However, the difficulty Mugabe and ZANU-PF faced in 2013 was the sense that they had betrayed this legacy. They recognised this and deliberately set out to change it, managing to achieve a reconnection with voters to a remarkable extent. A group of MDC activists discussed ZANU-PF's attempts to reconnect:

> ZANU managed to mend relationships.
> He pretended.
> No they mended.[47]

People were extremely grateful for the president's call for a peaceful election: 'For the first time, ZANU stayed away from violence. People

---

[45] Businessman, Harare, interviewed in Bulawayo, 9 November 2013 (JG).

[46] NGO head, Mashonaland Central, 14 November 2013 (JG).

[47] Exchange between two MDC-N activists, Bulawayo 9 November 2013 (JG).

were joining them willingly because of that.'[48] As already outlined, the party was vigorous in getting out to meet people, to listen to their concerns and to recognise them with gifts. One staunch MDC activist said: 'ZANU-PF, if they change their behaviour, and their name, maybe people will work for them. Maybe even I would.'[49] There was a sense that the party's desire to change was genuine, and that this had turned it back into the popular party of independence. One experienced civil society activist who has criticised the government's violence and mismanagement for years said:

> ZANU is reforming. It is genuine. One thing I have learned about Robert Mugabe is that the man is British at heart. He is a man of his word. He realises he is coming to the end of his rule and life. He wants to be remembered as someone who brokered peace and development. He is desperate for legitimacy and to succeed beyond what has been achieved by other African leaders.[50]

In these elections some Zimbabweans revealed the sense of loss they have lived with since things went wrong. Nostalgia had a part to play in this election: it represented an opportunity for some to re-engage with the president and state that had been lost to them. For some voters, this felt like a homecoming.

As our breakfast ended, the Harare businessman summed up the mass return to ZANU-PF.

> My uncle is a very strong MDC man. He was a war vet, spent 20 years in Zambia. He hates ZANU-PF. He told me he voted but it was the most painful moment of his life. The MDC never came. The area is where [former Vice President] Joice Mujuru is from. She came. She asked what were the issues. She saw the hospital which has no supplies or doctors, the bad roads, the lack of jobs. And she said, sorry, we have let you down. We will try to do better. And she

---

[48] MDC-N activists, Bulawayo 9 November 2013 (JG).
[49] MDC-T activist, Matabeleland South 10 November 2013 (JG).
[50] Civil society leader, Harare, 4 November 2013 (JG).

gave them maize. My uncle saw a young boy who was giving out MDC t-shirts being intimidated by a ZANU supporter. And a policeman came and stopped him. And my uncle was so impressed. And he thought, maybe we can return to our liberation, maybe we can give them one more chance. So he voted ZANU-PF.[51]

---

[51] Businessman, Harare, interviewed in Bulawayo, 9 November (JG).

6 Conflicting Reports and Assessments I

The Run-Up

In this chapter and the next we step back from the political players – elites and grass roots – to consider a number of key reports and statements leading up to and published in the aftermath of the 2013 elections. It is fair to say that few elections have received such scrutiny, underlined by such anxiety. In that sense, it was an extremely public set of elections attracting global attention. The sheer messiness of the 2008 elections, their violence and their far-from-credible final results cast a shadow over how the 2013 edition would be conducted. The elections in Kenya in March 2013, following upon the extremely violent and controversial elections of 2007 – and the coalition government that was subsequently brokered by Kofi Anan – resulted not only in a gracious acceptance of defeat by one of the two leading candidates, but was noted for its peacefulness and credibility. 'Peaceful and credible' became a vocabulary of acceptability, a level removed – some would say downwards – from 'free and fair'. In the reports that preceded and followed the Zimbabwean elections of 2013, these four terms would achieve great resonance, and the ways they were combined – and the ways in which one or other of the terms would be omitted – became key levers in a debate which runs to this day.

The term 'peaceful and credible' was first used by UN Secretary-General Ban Ki-moon, on 27 February 2013, as he urged Kenyan political leaders to conduct an election that would merit such a description.[1] The Kenyan leaders took his term seriously – certainly in the pains all sides took to keep the contest peaceful. The

---

[1] www.un.org/apps/news/story.asp?NewsID=44243#.VU5FG45Viko 27 February 2013, [cited 26 June 2015].

concession of defeat by the victor's main rival made it credible. For Zimbabwe's ZANU-PF, the term was a guide to its approach to the election to come.

Two key points should be made at the outset: first, the reports and prognoses, warnings, caveats and predictions began some time before the elections, and we take 2011 as a seminal year for such writing; second, it became not only reports about the elections, but also elections about the reports. That is, the reports so conditioned ZANU-PF's preparations for the elections that much strategic thinking was devoted to how the elections would be received – both by the authors of key reports and the observer groups who would be given accreditation, not to mention the host of journalists and scholars from all over the world who would be present. Through their responses and verdicts, governments around the world would be influenced – at least to the extent, perhaps, of tempering hitherto critical or even hostile views of ZANU-PF's Zimbabwe.

During 2011, it became clear to many that the coalition government was not working in the MDC's favour. By that is not meant any judgment to do with the MDC's being overshadowed or harassed by ZANU-PF – there was a continuous if largely low-level harassment and a series of hurdles for the MDC to navigate – but to do with Morgan Tsvangirai's ability as a Prime Minister, and the MDC MPs' capacities as Parliamentarians, notwithstanding those hurdles and harassments. There was no Parliamentary legislative programme, and the Prime Minister seemed to have no strategy. Caught up in the mire of a distorted and underfunded public administration, the MDC began to look like another part of the same furniture of malfunction. Tendai Biti's stabilisation of the economy by use primarily of the US dollar was exceptional – but a stabilised economy was still far from a prosperous one, or one that provided a foundation for future prosperity. It simply let people get their breath back after an epoch of horrendous hyper-inflation.

2011 was the year when people began to focus on the 2013 elections. This was made clear in the first two of the prognoses we shall look at. They were authored by two highly distinguished and knowledgeable observers of things Zimbabwean, Sue Onslow of the London School of Economics and Greg Mills of South Africa's Brenthurst Foundation. The Onslow paper of March 2011 was bleak in terms of her analysis of how far external actors would be able to impose themselves upon the Zimbabwean dynamic. The Thabo Mbeki-led negotiations towards a coalition government in 2008 had been an exception. The term 'dynamic' is our own, and suggests a political life force that is entirely Zimbabwean, self-generating and adaptable. It is able to be influenced, but not directed. Onslow suggests strong ideological animations for this dynamic that had by 2011 also dictated the terms of opposition discourse. This discourse had to be a response to a ZANU-PF liberation ethos and its ideological expression; an original or alternative MDC discourse would be very difficult. In other words, talk of change for the future was always countermanded by claims that the future could only be built on a past that had first been won by ZANU-PF. It had been won before there was an MDC, and the leader of the MDC had neither won it nor fought to win it. If he was not a quisling of the colonial powers, he had been a bystander.

The term 'patriotic history' was coined by Terence Ranger (2004) and taken forward by Miles Tendi (2010). In the Zimbabwean context it connoted a sole history, beyond an official history with possible unofficial readings and interpretations. Onslow notes that 'a wide spectrum of Zimbabwean intellectuals was involved in the elaboration and presentation of this patriotic history', but that it was a process that achieved full momentum from the late 1990s 'as a direct product of the emerging alliance between ZANU-PF and the war veterans'. Even so, it was an exaggerated history, as liberation was not fully won on the battlefield, but negotiated 'under enormous international pressure' at Lancaster House in late 1979 (Onslow, 2011: 5–6). But, given that 30–80,000 people had died in that liberation war, the claims to a patriotic history were not refuted. The very same history – one of violence – sanctioned further violence in the years of independence. So the key question Onslow asked was 'how far is ZANU-PF adapting to democratic politics?'

Here, her answer seems surprising in the first instance. Given its command of violence, ZANU-PF accommodated itself very studiously to the coalition government of 2008. That should be read with a note of caution as, even though ideologically united, ZANU-PF contained divisions about the extent to which pragmatism should be pursued. That has solidified and been expressed in the post-2013-election pogroms within the party. But, leading up to 2013, the key difference was over when those elections should be held and how solid party structures should be by the time of the elections. Having said that, the fact that both 'pragmatists' and 'hard-liners' within ZANU-PF agreed on a campaign platform of 'indigenisation and empowerment' suggests an ideological unity and a commitment to the same nationalist project. Where the so-called pragmatists were successful was in persuading the party as a whole to strengthen its grass-roots party apparatus. ZANU-PF MPs were encouraged to spend time in their constituencies and benefits to ZANU-PF areas were facilitated. The voting machine – the party's capacity to wheel out the voters – was strengthened and so was its capacity for psychological intimidation. This became more important than physical intimidation, and was conducted subtly but widely in the rural areas. At the same time, the military command structure, the Joint Operations Command, lurked as background power brokers. The army was by 2000 thoroughly politicised as a ZANU-PF machine, but was also divided on the need for violence or otherwise, and on what levels of violence might be required. In the event, the military was not called upon to exercise its brand of organised and coordinated violence because, as the economy and public administration struggled to recover, military personnel took increasingly large roles in running 'the crumbling infrastructure of the country and parastatal organizations' (Onslow, 2011: 2).[2] What this meant was, notwithstanding a

---

[2] Here Onslow cites similar views from Martin Rupiya (2007) and Knox Chitiyo (2009).

coalition government, ZANU-PF embedded itself as an organisational apparatus more strongly than ever in the countryside, the military, and key aspects of public administration. It also remained in strength as part of government, and in many ways a dominant part of what was meant to be a coalition government. The MDC had some reasonably large, but not dominant, parts of government – and some urban party apparatus. Even so, it was enough for the ZANU-PF pragmatists to have among their options the possibility of a post-2013 continuation of coalition – whereas the hawks sought outright victory.

The point is that no ZANU-PF faction at any time contemplated defeat, and the party organised accordingly. ZANU-PF adapted to the need for a democratic exercise – an election – to decide the future of politics, and adapted in a way that was more thorough, more systematic, and more subtle than in 2008.

The report by Greg Mills has similarities to that by Onslow. In particular, he contemplates the options open to the international as well as national actors. Those hoping to have major effect on ZANU-PF faced very limited options. Those of the Western nations boiled down to an emphasis on the proper conduct of the 2013 elections – preferably via multilateral action in the UN Security Council (Mills, 2011: 16). That would be unlikely. Otherwise, Mills suggests that the suspension of sanctions would have been wise, in that they simply gave ZANU-PF a ready-made excuse for its own failings – everything that was wrong with the country was because of the West.

For the SADC states, and South Africa in particular, the only viable option – since it was South Africa that brokered the coalition government – would be to see the coalition through to its end and seek to manage the conduct of the ensuing election. For the MDC, it could only do one of three things. It could stick to the coalition and, within it, seek to reform Mugabe and ZANU-PF. It could leave the coalition and go it alone in preparation for the elections – but risk doing so without the support of SADC. Or it could leave the coalition and go for mass action, but that would be uncertain and would certainly not gain the support of a SADC that had invested so heavily in facilitating the coalition and the idea of a cooperative, as opposed to confrontational, process (Ibid.: 17–20).

As it was, the MDC appeared unable to contemplate any but the first option. The behaviour of many of its senior members had become indistinguishable from that of ZANU-PF in terms of corrupt behavior and luxurious habits. The problem was that sticking to the coalition until the end of its term was the easy part. Reforming Mugabe when the need was also to reform itself was much more difficult. Mills cites correspondence he had received about such behaviour. 'The string of such indiscretions on the MDC side is much worse than is publicly known and "it's already longer than your arm – and the party hasn't even experienced unfettered power yet"' (Ibid.: 21).

The problem was a simple one: if all these things were known to outside observers, how much more might they have been known by citizens – either by observation or from the welter of internet sources readily accessible from Zimbabwe? There is a vibrant electronic press both within and outside the country, dedicated to Zimbabwean politics. The advent of smart phones in even the most remote areas, and good broadband coverage, has led to an information and opinion bonanza. It is more extensive than what is available in South Africa. It is so extensive, so pervasive, that in the 2013 elections the MDC were permitted to campaign in the rural areas. Nothing could be hidden from people anymore, no matter where they were. ZANU-PF, as noted earlier, had prepared an extremely strong rural campaigning apparatus, complete with psychological weaponry – and the MDC had not. Brief campaigning stops over a short space of time would change nothing. The MDC concentrated on its urban strongholds but, as discussed earlier in this book, did so haphazardly. Assuming that there was a greater concentration of educated voters and middle-class voters in the urban areas, their awareness of what Onslow and Mills were describing would be appreciable. Zimbabwe has always had a sophisticated electorate – and, in 2013, this sophistication was likely to lead to highly pragmatic and self-interested behaviour.

It is against this background that we now come to the key document that preceded the elections – the survey of voter intentions conducted by Susan Booysen and published by Freedom House. The MDC and others discounted its findings, emphasising the large number of 'undecideds' in terms of voting intentions. ZANU-PF would have looked at it very closely and modeled aspects of its final electoral strategy upon its data.[3]

THE BOOYSEN REPORT

Booysen, a South African-based academic, published her interim report in August 2012. It was based on a nationwide survey conducted in June and July of that year, and was the most intensive and in-depth survey of its kind in Zimbabwe. There was an achieved sample of 1,198, with a margin of error of plus or minus 2.8 per cent, covering 100 areas (63 rural and 37 urban, consistent with national population spread). In each area, 12 interviews were held, alternating male and female respondents (Booysen, 2012: 11).

Almost all senior diplomatic and MDC figures to whom I (SC) spoke during fieldwork – and I raised this in every one of my five visits between the release of the reports and the elections – dismissed the importance of the report for purposes of electoral projections. They did so because the report was published a year before 2013 elections, during which time much was projected to happen. The report was most strongly discounted as important for electoral projections – and hence electoral strategy within the MDC – because a total of 47 per cent of the respondents declined to declare their voting intentions (Ibid.: 5). This was interpreted by a senior MDC figure as representing an electorate with 47 per cent as 'undecideds'. Therefore there was much for which to campaign.[4] There seemed to be no further interrogation of the report's findings beyond this headline figure.

This was unfortunate in terms of the MDC's recognition of its position, as even the Executive Summary of an admittedly long and

[3] Senior ZANU-PF source (SC).   [4] Senior MDC official, Harare, March 2013 (SC).

densely detailed 'interim' report made telling points: a fall in MDC parliamentary vote between 2010 and 2012 from 38 to 20 per cent, while ZANU-PF achieved a growth in support over this period from 17 to 31 per cent (Ibid.). Booysen's report unveiled, over a series of carefully calibrated survey topics, a more detailed picture behind these gross figures. Here, we outline some of them – not to discuss them in deep detail, but to suggest that a year before the elections there was material for MDC strategists to contemplate. It is our suggestion that ZANU-PF strategists did – notwithstanding a response to us that consisted in an articulate knowing smile and brief replies: 'Have you studied the Booysen report?' Smiling: 'Yes, of course.' 'And?' Still smiling: 'We can build on this.'[5]

The executive summary, itself a four-and-a-half-page document, goes on to say that the coalition government – from which the MDC might have expected credit for stabilisation of the economy – was in 2012 perceived as less to the credit of the MDC than was felt in 2010. In 2010, 52 per cent considered the MDC as deserving the most credit for coalition success, but this figure fell in 2012 to 15 per cent. Not all of this drop became a ZANU-PF gain (Booysen, 2012: 7). At the very least, it suggested that the MDC was not articulating its message in a sustained way and that the 'bounce' people felt with a stabilised economy was not felt any more in an economy which was not in a position to achieve major growth or 'lift-off'. The question then became one of who could be seen as promising the greater 'lift-off' into the future?

Coming onto the main body of the report, Booysen noted a degree of optimism about the future. This was expressed as a sense of overall national prospects being positive, but of deep worry about personal finances and possibilities. The electorate, it might be thought, therefore wanted a continuation of national growth, but deliberately targeted policies to do with personal income and prospects. The report, however, revealed disturbing trends in party

---

[5] Senior ZANU-PF official, Harare, November 2012 (SC).

support, suggesting it was not the MDC which was seen as having either the best performance or performance capacities for the future.

In table three, under questions to do with what voters would do in the event of an immediate election (in 2012), preferences for the MDC, which in 2009 had been 55 per cent for the Presidency and in 2010 38 per cent in parliamentary elections, fell to 18 per cent for the Presidency and 20 per cent for Parliament. By contrast, in the same table, preferences for ZANU-PF in the 2009 Presidential stakes were 12 per cent, and in the 2010 parliamentary elections 17 per cent; these rose to 31 per cent for both President and Parliament.

Broken down across all provinces, the figures were worrisome for the MDC. Here we concentrate only on the major cities, long considered MDC strongholds. Again, the comparable years were 2010 and a hypothetical immediate 2012 election. In Harare, MDC support fell from 50 per cent to 17 per cent. ZANU-PF support rose from 8 per cent to 22 per cent. In Bulawayo, MDC support fell from 51 per cent to 29 per cent. ZANU-PF support rose from 4 per cent to 15 per cent. In the Midlands Province, seat of the city Gweru, MDC support fell from 36 per cent to 25 per cent, and ZANU-PF support rose from 19 per cent to 29 per cent. And in Manicaland province, seat of the city Mutare – and a province long regarded as a spiritual homeland for liberation, as militarised revolt against white rule first erupted there – MDC support fell from 40 per cent to 31 per cent and ZANU-PF support rose from 17 per cent to 34 per cent.

Table five was a revealing one to do with trust. From 2010 to 2012, 'a lot' of trust in the MDC fell from 32 per cent to 20 per cent and that in ZANU-PF rose from 16 per cent to 34 per cent (Booysen, 2012: tables 3–5: 18–20).

In terms of policy issues, respondent preferences at one level accorded with expectations. The MDC won most 'strongly agree' preferences on issues to do with (1) being less corrupt, (2) bringing change, (3) delivering services (especially at local level), and (4) civil liberties. ZANU-PF won most preferences on issues to do with (1) land reform, (2) indigenisation, (3) resistance to foreign intervention and (4) liberation. However, in the 'agree' column ZANU-PF was much closer to the MDC in all its areas of core strength, and surpassed the MDC by 29 per cent to 22 per cent in the area of being capable of bringing change (Ibid.: table six: 22). If this suggested that there could be a middle ground to play for, then our own findings in earlier chapters suggest that it was ZANU-PF that went after and largely secured such middle ground.

The acid test was of course performance to date within the coalition government. Here the reversals were startling. From 2010 to 2012, respondents viewed the success of the coalition as due more to one party or the other. In 2010, its success was seen as more due to the MDC by 53 per cent. In 2012, this had dropped to 15 per cent. By contrast, the success of the coalition seen as owing more to ZANU-PF rose from 13 per cent to only 16 per cent – the difference being ascribed to a view of equal contributions from both parties and this rose from 24 per cent in 2010 to 36 per cent (Ibid.: table 12: 31).

This suggests (a) the MDC lost support, but (b) ZANU-PF could not fully exploit this up to 2012. It did leave much to play for between 2012 and 2013 by both parties. Relating this to questions on trust was revealing precisely in terms of capturing or recapturing ground for 2013. 'A lot' of trust was reposed in 2012 in ZANU-PF by 24 per cent and only 16 per cent in the MDC. However, trust that existed 'not at all', or 'just a little', or attracted a 'don't know', amounted to just shy of 50 per cent for each of the two coalition parties, and in the coalition government as a whole (Ibid.: table 13: 32).

Broken down into trust for key offices of state, 'a lot' of trust in the Office of the President rose from 19 to 42 per cent, but that in the Office of the Prime Minister fell from 30 to 26 per cent. However, trust as being 'somewhat' present in the Office of the Prime Minister fell from 37 to 22 per cent, and in the Office of the President from 24 to 16 per cent (Ibid.: table 14: 33). This again suggested the need for campaign strategies to do with the 'marketing' of trust by both parties, but the higher end of trust, a sense of certainty about trust in Morgan Tsvangirai, should have become a paramount objective of MDC campaign preparation and public relations. To be sure, the survey questions were to do with offices of state and not directly about incumbency. Even so, those offices were associated with very well-known incumbents, and it is suggested that this was refracted in the survey responses. Less contentiously, the Office of Prime Minister did not seem to command huge confidence – making the Presidency, and trust in political figures as Presidential material, things that were key.

There is one aspect of the survey which we do wish to question, and that is the section to do with information gleaned from online sources. The survey found that such sources constituted only a tiny per cent of information feed among their respondents. In 2012, 3 per cent was the highest, and that was for the online edition of the pro-ZANU-PF paper, *The Herald*. Independent papers gleaned only 1 per cent (Ibid.: 45). Our word of caution is three-fold. First, the respondents were surveyed only on information from local web sources, and not information from South African, other regional and international sources such as the BBC. Second, our own fieldwork discussions suggested that use of such sources did increase as the elections drew closer. And third, the survey was unable to anticipate the Facebook phenomenon of *Baba Jukwa*, whose salacious and 'insider' daily posts became a subject of discussion wherever we went, and which intensified as polling day loomed. Chief among the discussions of *Baba Jukwa* was the question, 'where does he get his information from?' It seemed clearly a page published by a ZANU-PF insider with rogue tendencies. Although, right at the end, *Baba Jukwa* urged his friends and followers to vote MDC, it seemed to many that the future battles would be within ZANU-PF itself.

COUNTING DOWN TO THE ELECTIONS

There were five preoccupations on the part of observers, pundits and key civil society actors as the elections loomed. The first was that the SADC conditions, established after the 2008 elections for a free contest had not been fully honoured, and were not likely to be, and that this had been due to ZANU-PF intransigence or delaying tactics. The second was that ZANU-PF was a vehicle for Mugabe-ism, was in Mugabe's thrall, and would be relentless in securing his re-election. The third was that the election was unlikely to be as violent as that of 2008, but that the outcome, if it favoured Mugabe and ZANU-PF, would likely be contested on grounds of electoral freeness and fairness. The fourth was that, notwithstanding all these things, the MDC was not strong enough to win – but that ZANU-PF might not win outright either. And the fifth, accordingly, was speculation to do with a possible second coalition government.

The first of these, that key SADC conditions had not been observed was a key thrust of a document released by the SAPES Policy Dialogue Forum on 30 July, the eve of the election. However, the document made special note of the state of the voters' roll.

1. There was a large discrepancy between the number of people on the roll and the numbers indicated for each constituency.
2. There was a very large number of young people under 30 who were not registered as voters.
3. There was a large difference in rural registration compared to urban registration of voters, with the rural areas having a greater percentage of registrations and with a seeming bias towards the registration of older voters. (SAPES, 2013: 2)

The state of the voters' roll, or electoral register, would haunt both the elections and their aftermath. However, the greater registration of voters in the rural areas, compared to the urban areas, and older ones compared to younger ones, suggested a rural concentration of strength and possible manipulation there – with the possibility of older voters needing 'help' to vote – and a diminution of what might be seen as an MDC strength, that is, in younger urban voters.

The second point of Mugabe-ism was the thrust of an essay by the journalist-in-exile Wilfred Mhanda. He indicated that Mugabe had 'progressively sidelined and marginalised fellow struggle stalwarts ever since he got the helm of ZANU in January 1977 and packed the leadership structures of both the party and government' with those who either supported him or could not oppose him (Mhanda, 2011: 4).

His sense of Mugabe-ism would certainly be graphically illustrated in the aftermath to the elections.

The third to fifth points were the subject of overarching critiques of the electoral process by three highly respected sources. The first of these was by the Canadian scholar resident in Johannesburg, David Moore (2013a), and was composed in a pungent and deliberately acerbic style. At best, he looked to an exercise in 'democracy-lite', as opposed to an authoritarianism that could express itself even in electoral practice. But he also noted the seemingly deliberate manner of Robert Mugabe's belittling attacks on the senior South African political figure Lindiwe Zulu, who had expressed concerns about the run-up to the elections. The implication here is that Mugabe's target was not so much Zulu, but her President, Jacob Zuma, and that Zuma's efforts to prevent a diplomatic spat in fact was seen to bring him closer to Mugabe. But the key question was of course 'how will the ruling party win again?' Moore discounted the level of violence in 2008 being repeated. 'Neither local nor regional legitimacy would allow that.' However, 'recent polls have indicated MDC slippage – being in (the coalition government), getting caught up in municipal corruption, and its leader's well-exposed private life have not helped. The election could come close to a tie' (Moore, 2013a). In the advent of another coalition, how militarised would it be? Emerson Mnangagwa was rumoured to have held high-level discussions with the most-senior generals. If not militarised, how would any deal look, with rumours abounding of ZANU-PF 'moderates' seeking a coalition? 'All parties could agree to fudge an election.' There was even thought in the Harare rumour mills that, in seeking a postponement of 31 July as an election date, the MDC was in fact seeking to establish sufficient agreement on a second coalition to obviate the need for elections at all. In the event, the elections took place, and the struggle between Mnangagwa's securocrats and the ZANU-PF 'moderates' also took place, but a little later.

On 29 July, Brian Raftopoulos's Solidarity Peace Trust placed the ball firmly in the SADC court to ensure the elections were held in a

reasonable manner. This was particularly so as the earlier SADC conditions for such elections had not been fully implemented. However,
Raftopoulos did note that the SADC effort from 2008 had been 'to
establish conditions for a generally acceptable election in Zimbabwe'
(Raftopoulos, 2013b). It had of course to be seen as an acceptable expression 'of the will of the people' – but the term 'acceptable' now entered
the lexicon of these elections alongside 'peaceful' and 'credible'.

The widest globally circulating eve-of-election report came
from the International Crisis Group (2013). It was subtitled, portent-
ously, *Mugabe's Last Stand*. Its first paragraph declared the elections
'inadequately prepared ... Conditions for a free and fair vote do not
exist.' The report bemoaned the lack of fulfillment of the SADC
conditions and noted in particular that 'the voters roll is a shambles'.
There followed a lengthy indictment of ZANU-PF efforts to condition
the election in its favour, but the weight of the report was to be borne
by SADC and the African Union and their election observation teams.
'They must avoid a narrow technical approach.' But, even here, the
fall-back position was expressive. In the event of a 'deeply flawed'
vote, the observer groups should deem it illegitimate and press for a
re-run after some months of 'careful preparation' of an objective sort –
not dominated by a single party. There was an alternative immediately suggested, if a re-run was not possible, and that was to 'facilitate
negotiation of a compromise acceptable to the major parties' (International Crisis Group, 2013).

Towards the end of the report, the call was again made to the
observers to 'not fall back on a purely technical assessment of 31 July.
Their own election guidelines empower them to take a wide-angle
perspective' (Ibid.: 7). In the event, as we shall see, the observer groups
did take a 'wide-angle perspective', although it may not have been the
sort the International Crisis Group (ICG) authors had in mind. Even
so, the ICG report concluded that 'the least likely outcome is an
uncontested victory by either MDC-T or ZANU-PF'.

Four possible scenarios were posited: the first was ZANU-PF
winning 'a deeply flawed election that is accepted by most in the

interest of avoiding violence and further economic chaos'. The second was ZANU-PF winning 'a deeply flawed election that is accepted by SADC/AU observers, but not by MDC formations and civil society, leading to political impasse and economic deterioration'. The third was ZANU-PF winning a 'clearly rigged election', followed by unrest, repression and its consequences. And the fourth was the MDC winning at least a first-round victory, prompting a ZANU-PF hardliner's backlash before a second round. In fact, the outcome was a hybrid of the first two scenarios, but with the response of the MDC and civic action groups being curiously lacking in bite, and failing to garner extensive local or international support. We have given our fieldwork findings on the local reasons for this.

Once again, in the face of a possible impasse, the ICG called for a 'political solution involving a negotiated reconfiguration of power sharing' and, while this was negotiated, 'SADC and the AU should continue to recognize the current (coalition government) power-sharing administration as the legitimate government'. If both parties failed to agree on an election re-run, in the event one was required, 'an extension' of the coalition government, or variation of it 'would be required' (Ibid.: 9–10).

The difficulty with the ICG report was that it seemed to view coalition as the most preferable of evils – so much so that it became a default option if the virtues of democracy were not adopted. In a sense, it was a default view that valued the relative stability that coalition had brought Zimbabwe. In another sense, it seemed to express the idea that, for the MDC, its own outlooks were for either a controversial electoral defeat or coalition. None of the reports before the elections posited an MDC victory. They cited ZANU-PF obstacles to an MDC victory, but no report spoke of an MDC programme that inspired the electorate, or an MDC performance in government that excited the electorate. For the MDC, despite its hopes, its outlooks – if based on the prognoses of others – were at best tepid.

7   Conflicting Reports and Assessments II

The Aftermath

The results of the election were a disaster for MDC hopes. It was reduced from being a party of government to an opposition without any key leverage on issues of constitutional import. It became the kind of visible but polite opposition seen in countries like Singapore, Malaysia and Russia – evidence of sorts for 'democracy', allowed a certain amount of vocal space, shown off to a curious form of 'electoral tourism', but firmly in its relatively unimportant space.

The former Prime Minister, about to become leader of what shortly became a divided opposition, Morgan Tsvangirai, even before the full results were announced, described the election as a 'huge farce', and the result 'null and void' (BBC, 2013a). Other interim judgements were not so emphatic, but were cautionary all the same. The Zimbabwe Human Rights NGO Forum posted the concerns of the Zimbabwe Election Support Network (ZESN), which had deployed 7,000 observers throughout all parts of the country. Its report is considered more deeply later in this chapter, but its preliminary comments were to do with the electoral register or voters roll. It considered some one million voters had been disenfranchised. This was especially a problem for urban voters (only 67.94 per cent of such voters had been registered) and voters were turned away for reasons of not being registered or seeking to vote in the wrong wards at 82 per cent of urban stations, compared to only 38 per cent of rural stations. No figures of those turned away were given at this stage. However, although processes on the day were 'smooth' – no attempts were made at 98 per cent of the stations to intimidate or influence officials, and ZANU-PF and MDC party agents validated the processes at 97 to 99 per cent of the stations where they were present – the ZESN nevertheless, based on a variety of factors but chiefly on its concerns over registration and voters turned away, urged 'observers and stakeholders to look below the surface as there are some grave issues that have arisen. All is not well' (Zimbabwe Human Rights NGO Forum, 2013). The problem was that, at this stage, the full results had not been announced, and the cautions expressed were the same as those expressed by civic action groups before the polls began. There was, throughout the process, the sense of a self-fulfilling prophecy. It may have been an accurate prophecy – or not. We shall examine in the next section of this chapter what the ZESN reported in its fuller consideration, and what other key observation groups reported. However, other reactions a week later were not so much cautionary as blunt in their assessments.

David Moore penned a response to the elections on 8 August and began by noting how, at what was thought to have been 'Zimbabwe's largest ever political rally, in Harare behind the Rainbow Towers', two days before actual polling, the MDC's hopes would have reached their peak (Moore, 2013b). One of us (SC) attended that rally and was impressed by the huge number of young supporters, resplendent in MDC party t-shirts and baseball hats. The question was whether, in surveying that mass of people, Morgan Tsvangirai and the MDC leadership wondered how many of them were registered voters – or whether they had late misgivings about their party not having mounted any sort of voter registration programme. Moore noted the 'flat-footed-ness' and 'hubris' which the MDC seemed to generate, perhaps from having been so close to the centre of power but unable finally to achieve the party's political objectives. He also noted the debilitating effect of faction fights, chiefly between Tendai Biti and younger members of the leadership. Like the ZESN, but more acerbically, he noted 'the fantastical voters roll' and the 'thousands of "assisted voters"'. But he also foresaw that proving that these factors produced a fraudulent election would 'take months if not years to verify'. Having said all that, he wound down his report with a stinging rebuke which could only have been aimed at Morgan Tsvangirai: 'Charismatic preaching does not match dedicated intelligence and hard electoral work that matches Obama's in calculated sophistication' (Ibid.).

Moore therefore became among the first to say in public that the elections had to an extent been lost by the MDC as much as won by ZANU-PF. Away from public eyes, however, the assessments were incisive. We were given access to a private memorandum penned for the European Union. It does three key things: the first admits to the concerns about the SADC conditions and the voters roll; the second speaks to the MDC failings; and the third itemises those dynamic factors that ZANU-PF put into its campaign – some sinister and others strategies and tactics that were certainly ruthless and 'hard-ball', but not uncommon in elections elsewhere. However, the memorandum begins by conceding that the question of the voters roll and other concerns had substance, but this 'does not fully explain the extent of ZANU-PF's success nor does it exonerate the MDC-T from political misjudgment'.[1] What the memorandum then does is to lay out ZANU-PF strengths and how these strengths were deployed in the election campaign. It states that:

- ZANU-PF deployed a coherent strategy over the five years since the last elections.
- It always took pains to project power, or at least never to appear weak.
- It took all opportunities to humiliate its adversaries.
- Its accommodations of SADC requirements were always partial and insincere.
- It commanded the key government portfolios required to relaunch its bid for political control.
- It also worked to maintain control of both the streets and the judiciary, the latter so that its action could not be challenged by Parliament.
- It controlled state media and projected its nationalist narrative constantly.
- It was certain the memory of violence in 2008 had not faded and that people were frightened of its repetition, so it kept up a background of intimidation through both youth groups and traditional rulers.
- It ensured benefits flowed to potential constituencies of support.

---

[1] Private memorandum to the European Union Representative in Zimbabwe, 11 August 2013.

It did all these things systematically, as well as delaying the release of the voters roll while it worked to increase rural registration and that of the elderly, while discouraging any intense effort at urban registration and certainly at urban youth registration. Even so, the memorandum asks:

> Even while taking into account the difficult environment within which the MDC has had to operate, the failure to defeat an octogenarian who has destroyed the country's economy, pauperized its population, undermined all the country's institutions, and robs people of their fundamental political rights, beggars belief. Notwithstanding all the manipulation, the overt and subtle intimidation, and the accusations of some double voting, MDC-T must explain (to itself, in the first place) why it was that so many people voted for Mugabe? Could it also be put down to a lack of confidence in or enthusiasm for MDC-T and its leadership among voters?

The memorandum takes up a question from the Zimbabwe Human Rights NGO Forum: 'The question now is, should Zimbabwe's future be determined by information-starved folk who live in information-starved ghettos of fear and propaganda or should it be decided by well-informed citizens, especially the younger generation in urban areas?' The memorandum suggests that 'this can be read to suggest that poor rural people, because of the oppressive nature of society, should not be permitted to vote'. Apart from the condescension involved, the memorandum reminds the Forum that all communities have relatives in the urban areas, many have relatives in the diaspora, and that 'there is a good deal of interaction with the outside world and information exchange even in remote areas'. 'Rural folk' do not 'live in a hermetically sealed environment'. As we have tried to suggest, there was a range of highly rational and pragmatic reasons offered to us as to why voters cast their ballots the way they did. The memorandum suggests that the Forum's statement 'serves to underline the deep sense of shock and confusion in the NGO community'.

Notwithstanding this frank judgment, there were two key considerations that could not be dismissed. One was indeed the question of the electoral register and the advantage it seemed to give ZANU-PF. The second was the need to demonstrate its effects in terms of producing a wrong election result. As David Moore indicated, it would take perhaps years of court challenges to argue the case, and this would likely have to be done instance by instance or ward by ward. The ZESN, in its full report discussed next, outlined numerically the possible distortion of the election, but offered a strongly circumstantial case, rather than a conclusive one. The SADC and African Union (AU) reports could, in part, be taken to work on the premise that a result was needed, and had therefore to be validated, in order to prevent years of challenge and instability. This is where the use of vocabulary became paramount. However, the full ZESN report was at least no longer one of 'shock and confusion', but was sober and sombre.

THE OBSERVERS' REPORTS

The full report by the ZESN is the longest of all the major reports and goes out of its way to set everything in perspective. There is much historical detailing, but the report makes a very important contribution on the debate over the voters roll by providing comparative statistics on voter registration as against census population figures, and on how the Zimbabwe figures for youth registration compared with those in two surrounding countries and Kenya.

In South Africa, in 2009, 16.50 per cent of those between 18 and 25 were registered voters. In Zambia, in 2011, 20.61 per cent of those between 18 and 24 were registered. And, in Kenya, in 2013, 16.86 per cent of those between 18 and 25 were registered. These figures suggest there is a general problem in attaining high percentages of youth registration. However, in Zimbabwe, for the 2013 elections, only 4.51 per cent of those between 18 and 25 were registered – about a quarter of the percentages attained elsewhere (ZESN, 2013: 33–4). There were either more effective voter registration programmes elsewhere, or less effort to minimise youth voter registration, or a combination of those things.

Those registered to vote in Zimbabwe who were between 18 and 22 constituted only 2.39 per cent of the total roll, whereas that age group constituted 18.24 per cent of the population. Those between 23 and 29, constituted 11.37 per cent of the roll, but 22.97 per cent of the population. These figures indicate clearly that youth voters were very under-represented in terms of their population share. The percentages for those between 60 and over 80 were low in terms of total voter registration, but higher than total census population estimates for their age groups, for example 323,913 voters between 70 and 79 were registered, while there were by census estimate only 246,784 such people alive.

This was either because of the invention of false registrations, or chaotic registration overall – the problem being perhaps not so much new registrations but the failure to remove old ones that were no longer current. In every age range from 30 upwards to over 80, more people were registered than were alive in Zimbabwe. Those between 30 and 49 constituted just over 50 per cent of the registered electorate – so this should have been the central ground for electoral contestation, with the young and the elderly contributing critical marginal votes – but they may also have constituted marginal variables in terms of the suspicions of many observers. Both youth registrations and elderly registrations showed urban/rural differentials. Percentages of registrations were consistently higher in rural wards. However, in the critical middle ground, registration of those between 30 and 49 constituted 60 per cent of the urban roll, whereas they constituted 47 per cent of the rural roll (Ibid.: 33, 35).

Even so, in the 'uses' of the elderly vote, or what was assumed to be the elderly vote, there was 'assisted voting' at 49 per cent of rural stations, and only 5 per cent of urban stations. Total assisted voters constituted 5.9 per cent of those voting. Many voters were turned away for reasons that included appearing in the wrong ward or not being registered. They were 8.7 per cent of the total voting

(Ibid.: 61–2) – although it is unclear how many who came first to the wrong ward, and were turned away, subsequently found their right ward and were not turned away. Overall, one can say that the very small percentage of registered youth, the higher than actual population registration of elderly voters, and the large percentage of assisted votes in the rural areas, was deeply suspicious – but that should be set against the overall context that registration simply seemed to be a mess. We also do not know whether people were assisted to vote because of old age, or for other reasons such as illiteracy or bewilderment with the electoral process, were simply coaxed or coerced into being 'assisted' or elected to be assisted to ensure an alibi for their having voted 'correctly' (see Chapter 5).

The ZESN report noted the existence of radio stations broadcasting into Zimbabwe from abroad, and the 'increasingly significant' use of Facebook, Twitter and other platforms (Ibid.: 45).

The report contained a list of incidents at various polling stations, but they did not add up to a national picture of violations of electoral process. The report's list of non or partial fulfillment of SADC conditions for the election was an extremely helpful checklist (Ibid.: 77–80). But, even here, the terms 'improved', 'better', and 'no overt violence' suggested a flawed election that was at least better than that of 2008. The report did, however, argue that the SADC response to the elections as 'generally credible' could not be regarded as a term 'found in the (SADC) guidelines and is a vague description of the elections'. It argued that the SADC commendation of the elections as 'peaceful' was insufficient validation of the process, 'as peace is not the only criteria for a credible poll'. The overall ZESN conclusion was that the elections had indeed been 'relatively calm and peaceful', but that the various 'challenges' outlined in the report 'seriously compromised the credibility and fairness' of the elections (Ibid.: 80).

So, of the various terms mooted before the elections as possible validating labels – 'free and fair', 'peaceful and credible', 'acceptable' – the ZESN awarded the elections only a 'peaceful' label. It excluded 'credible' and 'fair', and did not mention 'free'. Since, however, it had challenged the SADC conclusion, it is to the SADC and then the AU reports that we shall now turn. These took, as intimated above, a more pragmatic approach, but not one without serious examination of what had occurred.

The full and final SADC report was published on 2 September 2013, and it built upon what were regarded as emphatic but controversial conclusions in the 2 August 2013 preliminary statement by the chairman of the 573 SADC observers, Bernard Kamillius Membe, the Tanzanian Minister of Foreign Affairs and International Cooperation. In particular, in that preliminary statement Membe said: 'In the main, the electoral process was characterized by an atmosphere of peace and political tolerance. Political parties and candidates were able to freely undertake their political activities unhindered.' The report viewed the election as a 'new chapter in the process of consolidation of democracy' in Zimbabwe, and called 'on all political parties to respect and accept the election results'. Membe's sign-off line was one of congratulations for 'free and peaceful' elections (SADC, 2013a). The attributes of 'peaceful', 'free', and 'acceptable' were here deployed. Missing at this stage were the attributes of 'fairness' and 'credibility'.

Membe returned to Zimbabwe from Tanzania to deliver the final report. As you may recall, the main message in the preliminary report was that the elections were free and peaceful. However, we had reserved the two issues of '"fairness and credibility"' (SADC, 2013b). Membe then reiterated that the elections had been free. 'Free in the sense that our observers noted that the candidates were free to campaign, free to associate, free to express their views and the voters were free to cast their votes. Because of that, we therefore concluded without hesitation that the harmonized elections were free and expressed the will of the people.' He also reiterated that the elections had been peaceful, and contrasted this with 2008.

However, on the matter of fairness, Membe noted that public broadcasting had not been made fairly available to the opposition parties, and, in particular, that 'the provision of the voters roll in time goes to the very heart of fairness in the election process. If the voters roll is not made available on time, the fairness of the election is brought into question.' The final SADC report, therefore, did not conclude that the elections had been 'fair'.

Had they been 'credible'? Membe said that, 'while agreeing that there were issues such as the delay of the voters roll and media polarization, there were so many other elements that when put together elevated the election to a credible status.' He reiterated the free electoral environment, the freedom of candidates and voters, the lack of intimidation during the polls, and the freedom of voting itself – and that all these things constituted 'the credibility under the prevailing circumstances, particularly when compared to the 2008 election'. On this basis – albeit somewhat contingent, more good than bad, and comparatively more good than 2008 – the elections were 'credible'. From SADC, therefore, came the vocabulary of 'peaceful', 'credible', 'acceptable', 'free' – but not 'fair'. If this seemed a pragmatism to the point of contortion, there was at least a reasoned argument for a verdict that looked at an imperfect exercise without regarding attributes such as 'free and fair' as pure virtues. Even so, the elections were not 'fair'.

The preliminary statement of the AU electoral mission, headed by former Nigerian President, Olusegun Obasanjo, declared the elections 'free, honest and credible' (BBC, 2013b). The use of the term 'free and fair' was, however, contingent, as Obasanjo said they had been free and fair 'from the campaigning point of view' (BBC, 2013c). He also said they had been 'credible' (SABC, 2013). These statements were taken as the AU endorsement of the electoral outcome. The final AU report, however, did not use any of these terms. It was an 82-paragraph document, with many sub-paragraphs, that narrated the background to the election; then listed in detail the complaints of the opposition leader, Morgan Tsvangirai, as expressed in an application to the Constitutional Court for nullification of the election results – together with the counter-arguments submitted in an affidavit to the Court by the Zimbabwe Electoral Commission. The Court's ruling was then given and the AU report concluded with a set of nine recommendations that suggested, in some key respects such as the availability of the voters roll, a not fully perfect election. However, it is the Tsvangirai application to the Constitutional Court, and the Electoral Commission's reply that excited the mission's particular interest (African Union Commission, 2013: pars. 77–80).

Tsvangirai petitioned to the Court that:

- The elections were unconstitutional in that the election date of 31 July had been chosen by President Mugabe without consultation.
- The closure of registration centres on 9 July rendered 750,000 potential registrants unable to register and thus deprived them of their voting rights.
- The late availability of the voters roll for searchable and analytic purposes violated provisions of the law.
- The voters roll contained 870,000 duplicate names. The Electoral Commission printed 2 million extra ballot papers, over and above the 6.4 million required for that number of registered voters, thus risking multiple voting infringements.
- Multiple voting was not credibly controlled in the Special Voting process (this was a process to allow police to vote) and there was a discrepancy between people eligible to vote under this scheme and the total number of police.
- Postal voting (this was designed for diplomats abroad) was made available too late for postal votes to be cast.
- While there was no overt physical violence, psychological violence characterised the elections.
- Assisted voters were 'assisted' under duress.
- Up to 750,000 voters were turned away from stations.
- Persons whose names were not on the voters roll were often allowed to vote.
- No information was provided on the ballots for Special Voting.
- Food relief was used as a means of bribery to purchase votes.
- The public media was highly biased against the opposition.

These complaints echoed those made by civic action groups, including the ZESN. The Electoral Commission replied to the Tsvangirai application; on the main points raised, it argued:

- The time frames for the election had been subject to the directives of the Constitutional Court.
- Mr Tsvangirai had not, in the period of preparation for the elections, indicated to the Electoral Commission that its measures 'were not in accordance to the holding of a free and fair election'.
- The closure of registration centres was at the end of a time frame of 30 days, earlier announced, and Mr Tsvangirai could not demonstrate and support with evidence how many eligible voters remained unregistered, nor how this detracted from the final results.
- The possible duplication of prospective registrants was due to the onward-going exercises in issuing identity cards, birth certificates, and replacement ID cards.
- Mr Tsvangirai could not demonstrate evidentially how many of his supporters had been disenfranchised, and how this detracted from the final results.
- The Electoral Court had earlier, in response to another MDC-T application, set out its logistical difficulties in producing the voters roll.
- Documents of duplicate names on the voters roll were dismissed by the Registrar-General of Voters as being not authentic. Mr Tsvangirai did not demonstrate how double voting might occur and why it would specifically disadvantage him and his party and not any other.
- Special Voters, even if they had voted twice, could not have materially influenced the outcome of the elections, as there were only 60,000 such approved voters and the President's majority was over one million.
- Mr Tsvangirai could not demonstrate how 200,000 assisted voters could be said to have voted only against him and his party.
- Nor could Mr Tsvangirai demonstrate how 750,000 voters were turned away, and that they would all have voted for him and his party. In areas where Mr Tsvangirai had won convincingly, for instance in Mashonaland West, 56,733 voters had been turned away, yet he still won convincingly. Mr Mugabe could perhaps make the same claim that those turned away might have voted for him and thus the MDC result would have been eroded.

Morgan Tsvangirai withdrew his petition to the Constitutional Court on 16 August 2013, citing the non-availability of election material. The Constitutional Court duly declared the elections 'free, fair and credible'.

The petition had been, however, lacking a firm evidential base from the outset. It was a hurried petition, and this was understandable given the compressed time frames available for such a petition to be lodged. But, quite apart from the verification of the numbers cited at that stage was the assumption that all those numbers cited as not registered or turned away would have voted MDC, and that all those assisted or given special votes would have voted ZANU-PF, and that was unsupportable in any legal context. However, having given room to the Tsvangirai arguments and the counter-arguments, the AU report, in its concluding recommendations, did specifically say that the voters roll should, in future, be made available for verification and inspection, both in electronic and hard forms, 14 days before the elections. 'The integrity of the Voters Roll must be assured through greater transparency, accessibility and public communications' (African Union Commission, 2013: par 82b). The AU cited other matters for improvement, such as better security markings on ballot papers to ensure non-duplication, but its remarks on the voters roll did, to an appreciable extent, chime with the concerns of the ZESN.

Even so, every officially invited external observer mission to the elections accepted the results. Even the ZESN, while issuing its concerns and cautions, called on Zimbabweans 'to ensure the holding of credible and fair elections in the future' (ZESN, 2013: 80) – suggesting that, for now at least, the 2013 election results, if not acceptable, had to be accepted.

ACADEMIC ANALYSIS

Academic literature on the 2013 elections focused on two main aspects: the strategies and effectiveness of the party elites, and the ways in which these interacted with international interests and actors, in SADC and in the West. Virtually none of it had anything to say about how voters reacted or participated in the elections. Booysen, whose analysis of the polling data collected over the life of the IG was published after the election, is a rare exception. She shows how the 'unimagined' turnaround in Zimbabwean politics should have been apparent to anyone who had followed the polls (2014: 54). They clearly demonstrate, as we have discussed, that popular trust and support for the MDC had drained steadily away between 2009 and 2012, while the ZANU-PF policies of indigenisation and land reform, the party's condemnation of foreign interference and articulation of a Zimbabwean identity shaped around the liberation struggle began to gain traction among voters.

Other accounts focus on the elites, assuming, perhaps, that there was little agency at the grass-roots level. Dewa and Makaye (2013), who explain the MDC crash as resulting from the lack of voter education, certainly reinforce the idea of the Zimbabwean electorate as junior players in the election drama.

Analysis of the election campaigns is fairly evenly spread between ZANU-PF and the MDC-T (there is scant mention of the MDC-N or ZAPU). There is a wide range of opinion between authors over how ZANU-PF achieved success. On one hand are authors who see ZANU-PF's victory as largely the outcome of cheating, intimidation and indoctrination. Dube and Makaye, for example, focus on the effects of rigging, describing gerrymandering, the manipulation of the voters roll, multiple voting, intimidation and the use of extra ballot papers, and conclude that '[o]ver and above everything, ZANU-PF engaged in a variety of electoral shenanigans that ensured its "resounding victory"' (2013: 33). Moore (2013a) makes a similar argument, detailing the cheating, coercion and populist strategies used to fool voters into supporting the ruling party. Two other academics, Bratton and Kibble, see the struggle as a largely top-down affair, characterised by raw power politics (Bratton, 2014) and intimidation and violence (Kibble, 2013). Looking at the election from the perspective of early 2013, Kibble argued that ZANU-PF was preparing for a dirty fight: 'Outright systemic physical violence has currently been replaced to some extent by intimidation and psychological violence amid a climate of fear … ZANU-PF lacks domestic and international legitimacy and has declining regional support. It also has decrepit party structures, massive unpopularity, and constant battle (sic) between factions as Mugabe refuses to nominate a successor' (Ibid.: 113).

But there are more complex analyses of how ZANU-PF used its position in the Inclusive Government (IG), its years of experience of electioneering, and its understanding of the electorate to run a professional and effective campaign. LeBas (2014), looking at the working of the IG, detailed the ways in which ZANU-PF had used the power-sharing arrangement to strengthen its own control of the country's security apparatus, and its patronage over poor urban residents through control of access to trading stands and house plots, all of which it was able to call on in 2013. Raftopoulos develops a similar analysis, explaining the imaginative and material hold ZANU-PF cultivated in the years before the election. The party built and maintained a 'substantial social base' built 'on a combination of the ideological legacies of the liberation struggle, the persistent memories of colonial dispossession, and the land reform process' (2013c: 979) along with a gradual absorption of the informal mining and trade sectors into its realm of patronage. Tendi, who followed the ZANU-PF campaign on the ground, writes of it as 'slick, well-funded, united and peaceful', a campaign in which very little was left to chance (2013: 963). Large resources were poured into creating spectacular rallies and to distributing food and party regalia. In sharp contrast with Kibble's predictions, Tendi describes a party that was loyal and energetic – he singles out Joice Mujuru as particularly effective and loyal, although she would later come unstuck in the post-election succession games. Crucial too, according to Tendi, was Mugabe's own mastery over the election: his wit, his energy and his effective use of the media during the campaign seem at odds with the more common image of a tired, sick, old man.

Several authors acknowledged the way ZANU-PF messages and policies resonated with the electorate. Southall discusses the attractiveness of its 'programmatic message' (2013: 137), particularly the indigenisation and land reform programmes. Messages based on patriotism and nationalism rooted in the party's historic engagement with the anti-colonial war were also attractive, and constantly reinforced through party messages and slogans about Western sanctions (Munaki, 2013).

The failure of the MDC is explored as closely. The bulk of the analysis focuses on the campaign itself – possibly because much of it represents a first attempt to explain the shocking turnaround of the party's fortunes and the campaign was the most immediate cause. Zamchiya (2013) gives intimate reflections on the campaign itself, having followed it at close hand. His account is one of a complacent leadership that refused to listen to the warnings of its own technical team. The party 'was blinded by ambition, suspicion of intellectuals, the animated atmosphere at political rallies, and a creeping sense of a divine ordination to govern' (2013: 956). Moreover, as Zamchiya notes, the party was heavily outspent by the ruling party, barely able to provide transport for its candidates (Ibid.: 961). Goredema and Chigora (2014) describe Tsvangirai's lack of rapport with voters, something seen in both his discomfort in personally engaging with them, and the incongruence of the party's policies. And Moore (2014), whose analysis largely puts ZANU-PF's victory down to 'chicanery', 'cheating' and 'populism', admits that the MDC was naively unprepared for the election.

But others look for more deep-seated reasons. Munaki (2013) argues that the MDC-T lost power because voters saw it as ineffective and corrupt in government – at national and local levels. LeBas explains how this perception came about through the party's engagement in the IG, within the 'perverse dynamics of power sharing in Zimbabwe' (2014: 53). Here, its organisational capacity and ability to maintain loyalty from its followers were effectively undermined by its own lack of experience and the manipulation of ZANU-PF. 'By abandoning the rhetoric and campaign platform that had built the party, the MDC-T contributed to the erosion of its grass-roots support and the growing apathy of its core activists' (Ibid.: 63). Raftopoulos explains that the MDC's discourse on democracy and neo-liberalism 'was always found wanting, against the redistributive logic of ZANU

(PF)'s land reform process, the ideological legacies of the liberation movement, and the discourse of state sovereignty' (2013c: 984). Over-all, the analysis adds up to a picture of a party with a superficial popular hold, fragmented and lost without the focus of political and economic crisis and the clear-cut distinctions of opposition.

Zimbabwe's domestic politics has been powerfully shaped by international relationships and the 2013 elections were no excep-tion. As has been the case in recent years, much of the political rhetoric focused on the main parties' relationship with the West. According to Tendi, Mugabe and his team saw winning in 2013 as an important victory over the West, almost as much as over the MDC. Humiliated by the 2008 results which he thought of 'as a victory for his western – British especially – detractors' (2013: 963), Mugabe saw 2013 as an opportunity to 'signal his final triumph over the west' (Ibid.: 964). For the MDC-T, Western backing now became a liability, as Mugabe successfully used the sanctions issue against them. As Munaki pointed out in the run-up to the polls: 'The reason why the MDC will not win is that they have turned against the people by calling for sanctions against Zimbabwe' (2013: 1).

There were other problematic international forces at work in 2013, outlined in particular by authors sympathetic to the opposition. The shadowy Israeli company Nikuv was highlighted by some as playing a key role in helping ZANU-PF fix the elections. Dube and Makaye for example describe a popular theory amongst opposition activists. Nikuv provided 'a delicate ballot paper [that] was used to rig the election ... [it had] a watermarked X against Mugabe and ZANU-PF's name such that if any ink was placed on the paper the substance on the paper would react and remove the ink and that activated the watermarked X into print' (2013: 37).

But the largest share of the discussion was devoted to the role of the SADC countries, in particular South Africa, and its president's equivocations on the conduct of the elections. Moore describes these as 'slippery' (2014: 60) but crucial, since international recognition of the elections and the regime they led to is the bedrock of regional and international legitimacy. Raftopoulos explains South Africa's failure to follow through on its threat to enforce free and fair elections, as the result of the need for regional stability: 'Guided by liberation movement solidarity with ZANU-PF and the need to stabilise the political situation with the support of the political-military establishment in Zimbabwe, Zuma blinked in the face of Mugabe's humiliating affront to South Africa, and SADC took what can only be described as a supine position on the electoral outcome' (2013c: 986).

However, this is understood as more than pragmatism, by Raftopoulos and others. Mahomva describes the elections as a legitimisation of 'Mugabeism' both regionally as well as domestically (2013: 3), seeing the election, its outcome, and its approval from the countries of the region as cementing a place for Mugabe's philosophy. Raftopoulos too describes how the election has led to a regional perspective on Zimbabwe as an 'anchor state', one that might serve as a role model and leader (2014: 97).

This is not a simple choice between the liberalism of the West and a position as a nationalist or indigenous vision of the country within the region. Raftopoulos (2014) argues that the 'desperate budgetary requirements of the state' contradict the government's desire to take up the role as a regional leader. This is an old story, according to Ncube (2013), echoing the dilemmas faced in the choice between competing human rights discourses: those of national self-determination versus liberal democracy. The first provides a domestic and regional anchor, connected to social and economic justice rights, while the second links Zimbabwe into global neoliberalism, including liberal property rights and an emphasis on political and civic rights. The 2013 elections, Ncube argues, violated liberal rights, but might have cemented a commitment to social rights. In the immediate term, at least, they 'solved the crisis of legitimacy' (2013: 107). But this outcome also helps explain why the 2013 elections were more acceptable in the region than they have been to the West.

DEVELOPING REFLECTIONS

Three things started happening after the elections: the MDC began a fractious debate and split; ZANU-PF, which one would have supposed was reinvigorated by its victory, also began a fractious process which led to the expulsions of very senior members – these matters are discussed later – and the assessments of the elections, given some months of reflection, began to assume a tone that was both sobering in its comments not only on the elections but on how 'ballpark' figures had been used to demonstrate that the elections had been 'fixed'. Since figures were always going to be the basis of future discussions and recriminations, it was left to Brian Raftopoulos to be the first to attempt the unpacking of these figures.

His Solidarity Peace Trust report of October 2013 – the second longest of the election reports, after that by the ZESN – began with a series of field testimonies from various voters. They chime very exactly with our own interviews and testimonies confided to us. 'Whoever wants a situation again like that of the 2008 elections?' 'You see food was used in campaigning and people had no choice … but to vote for that bucket of rice.' 'We lost on strategy, as technically ZANU-PF had an upper hand.' 'He (Tsvangirai) introduced the candidate he imposed.' '(Citing the late Joshua Nkomo, the rival liberation leader to Mugabe and an early opposition leader) I better join these people (ZANU-PF) so that we unite and I fix things internally' (Solidarity Peace Trust, 2013: 3–4). The reasons given by individual respondents on why they voted as they did formed a huge subtext to the overall figures that emerged from the elections. Raftopoulos, however, argues that the overall figures cannot reveal a further critical subtext, a determining one, and that is how the figures panned out at the local level, and how or whether they formed different patterns to the national figures.

20,000 independent observers were deployed throughout Zimbabwe during the elections, 9,000 of whom were drawn from Zimbabwean civic organisations. Every candidate was entitled to two polling agents at every single polling station, and in 96 per cent of these stations there were opposition agents. They were able to witness both the voting and the counting of the votes. 'Considering the large numbers of independent observers and polling agents, it is hard to explain why to date there are no systematic independent sources of voting statistics in the public domain down to the constituency and ward level countrywide, in particular with regard to assisted voters and voters turned away.' Neither the Electoral Commission nor the observers had provided this, so ballpark national figures were all that anchored the post-election debate (Ibid.: 31).

Raftopoulos thus set about providing at least some sets of more forensic figures. The Solidarity Peace Trust report noted that the split in the opposition groups, leading to competing opposition parties, cost the MDC 17 seats in 2013. With those 17, meaning 89 MDC seats or 33 per cent of the House, ZANU-PF would have needed every single one of its MPs present to pass changes to the constitution. The MDC would not have had quite a blocking third, but something very close to one. A united opposition would also have carried four provinces as opposed to two.

Although the overall popular vote showed a dramatic upswing for ZANU-PF in 2013, compared to 2008, that upswing is lessened when placed in the context of overall swings and fluctuations since 2002. Interestingly, ZANU-PF attracted more Parliamentary votes than Mugabe attracted Presidential votes in both 2008 and 2013, suggesting that President Mugabe was a little less popular than his party (Ibid.: 34–5).

But Morgan Tsvangirai also experienced fluctuations. Although he overwhelmingly took Bulawayo with 68 per cent of the votes, compared to Mugabe's 24 per cent, the total number of votes was slight. Tsvangirai took three times the number of votes in Harare as he did in Bulawayo, indicating a huge drop in electoral strength in his western strongholds – manifest either in disinterest or in population shifts away from the western regions. Outside the western provinces, only in Harare did Tsvangirai defeat Mugabe. In the Presidential stakes, even if all the votes attracted by a dissident MDC breakaway Presidential candidate, Welshman Ncube, had gone instead to Tsvangirai, Mugabe would still have handsomely won the Presidential elections. However, if Ncube's splinter MDC had not contested the western provinces, a united MDC would have 19 seats out of 26 – whereas, because of split opposition votes, ZANU-PF took 20 Parliamentary seats. In this sense, from the Solidarity Peace Trust report, the Parliamentary and Presidential elections deserved separate analyses and indicated a very complex election (Ibid.: 35–7).

Although constituency and ward figures for voters turned away are not available, provincial ones are. The provincial average is 7.4 per cent of those turning up to vote, although some provincial figures could be as low as 4.9 per cent. 15.2 per cent were turned away in Harare, an MDC stronghold – but 15 per cent were also turned away in Mashonaland West, a ZANU-PF stronghold. No comparative figures are available from previous elections.

In terms of assisted voting, there were 206,901 assisted voters nationwide, or 5.9 per cent of the voters. This seems ostensibly reasonable in a country where 14 per cent of the voters are considered illiterate. There were however many accounts of 'assistance' where it was neither requested nor welcomed (Ibid.: 38–40). Similarly, although there were numerous reports of 'bussing in' voters who seemed strangers to the constituency concerned, it is difficult to establish a scientific indication as to their effect – although Raftopoulos suggests it is reasonable to expect an effect when bussing-in is combined with percentages turned away in MDC strongholds, but no exact assessment is possible. But what this means is an opposition and civic action narrative based on broad figures and largely untabulated incidental accounts of coerced assistance or bussing-in. Raftopoulos concludes that the figures of the past five elections do not point to any opposition triumph in the 2018 elections:

> unless ZANU-PF itself faces dramatic internal challenges which shift the political landscape ... The socio-economic power base of

Zimbabwe has been significantly shifted to entrench a ZANU-PF elite and to ensure their support in rural and some urban areas via patronage and coercion, and the opposition needs to engage with this reality. Having a support base in Harare, other small urban areas and in three increasingly depopulating western provinces will not be sufficient to dislodge ZANU-PF ... The democratic movement needs to rebuild and restrategise, bearing in mind the need to engage in new ways with a dynamic and changing electorate, particularly in rural areas, resettled areas and in the informal mining sectors. These are all parts of the electorate where ZANU-PF, by whatever means, has convincingly captured the vote in this election. (Ibid.: 44–5)

The frustration expressed in this report, both towards an opposition that did not punch its weight and towards a ruling party which combined an accurate reading of the electorate with a blend of sophisticated and probably untoward electioneering, did not disguise the report's analysis – and this was that scientific evidence of election theft is not available. There was real skill and targeted policy agenda in the ZANU-PF campaign, and there was somewhat less skill and less targeted policy agenda in the MDC campaign.

It makes the 26 March 2015 conclusions by former Australian Ambassador to Zimbabwe, Matthew Neuhaus, seem out of kilter with evidence, although fully in kilter with suspicion and disappointment. Neuhaus disagrees with the aforementioned arguments. They suggested, in Neuhaus's reading, 'a fundamental shift back to ZANU-PF in political allegiance' (Neuhaus, 2015). In fact, that reading, like the one in this book, and consonant with that by Raftopoulos, has to do with a shift towards ZANU-PF because of pragmatism, self-interest, and disillusion with the MDC (see also Gallagher, 2015a).

Neuhaus is himself somewhat disillusioned with the MDC. He is highly critical of Tsvangirai and his coterie. He cites his own conversation with Tendai Biti, already embroiled in faction-fighting and now no longer involved with Morgan Tsvangirai. Biti's ascerbic aside to Neuhaus was bitter, and biting. 'Power corrupts, but the illusion of power corrupts even more.' Our own opinion of Tsvangirai is hard but more forgiving. One man cannot direct an entire party by himself. If he had wanted to, the party should have insisted on internal democracy. If that had been impossible, then even those who were most closely supportive of him should have studied their own electoral strategy more deeply. The fault lies with an entire party leadership as well as with its leader.

We return to Raftopoulos's caveat: the MDC will not win the 2018 elections 'unless ZANU-PF itself faces dramatic internal challenges'. Those challenges, as we shall relate, came speedily. Raftopoulos, returning in June 2014 to this theme, saw a desolate contradiction in place of a coherent ZANU-PF economic policy. An electoral policy of further and greater indigenisation, that is, a greater economic nationalism, could only work with greater foreign funding – and that was not in 2014 forthcoming. Instead, ZANU-PF was split between those seeking sufficient reforms to attract international assistance, and those who were set in their ways along the President's lines (Raftopoulos, 2014).

Before we engage these post-election matters, however, and with all the reports discussed in this chapter in mind, let us make some headline points.

- The first is that the MDC was wrong to discount the 47 per cent who declined to declare a party or voting preference in the Booysen survey. That headline figure did not mean that 47 per cent were undecided. Read in concert with the other figures in the Booysen document, it should have indicated worrying trends to the MDC strategists – but also given them key grounds upon which to construct a vote-attracting electoral platform.
- The second is that, in Parliamentary terms, the inability of Morgan Tsvangirai and Welshman Ncube to forge a unified opposition was extremely costly to MDC-Tsvangirai. The perception that Tsvangirai was slow, unwilling, or half-hearted in seeking to court Ncube was unhelpful when both men were campaigning for, in particular, votes in the western provinces.

- The third is that, again in Parliamentary terms, the activism of ZANU-PF MPs in courting and providing for their constituencies stood in contrast to the inaction of MDC MPs. The lifestyle of Morgan Tsvangirai – his multi-uxoriousness in particular – painted the picture of a man who had drifted from the people.
- The fourth is that, notwithstanding the huge rallies held by the MDC, particularly the final rally by the Rainbow Towers Hotel in Harare, in which many thousands of youthful supporters were in enthusiastic attendance, the MDC mounted no campaign to ensure these supporters were registered as voters.
- The fifth is the sobering calculation that, notwithstanding the batting backwards and forwards of figures, especially the numbers who had been disenfranchised by not being on the voters roll, and the numbers of assisted voters, it would have taken *all* those said to be unregistered, and *all* those who were assisted to vote, to have voted for Morgan Tsvangirai as President, for him to have narrowly defeated Robert Mugabe.

There are huge question marks over this election, but none of the verdicts to do with outright theft of the results can be sustained. The voters roll was a scandal, and all observer groups noted that. Varying combinations of the words 'free', 'fair', peaceful', 'credible' and 'acceptable' were used by these groups. Most concluded that the elections were not fully fair. 'Credible' was a disputed appellation and, even when applied, was applied with direct comparison to how much better, and therefore more credible, these elections were from those of 2008. 'Peaceful' achieved universal agreement, albeit with many noting a backdrop of psychological intimidation. It was 'free' in the weeks of campaigning and the days of polling – but there was a long gap between 2008 and 2013. This was a time when all manner of strategies could have been devised – fair, hardball but honest, hardball and dishonest – by ZANU-PF. It was also a time when the MDC could have prepared for elections more thoroughly and better informed than was the case. It was a time when ZANU-PF looked very hard at the electorate and, in one way or another, played to it. It was a time when the MDC did not.

The two longest and most detailed reports, by the ZESN and by the Solidarity Peace Trust, were impressive in their efforts to reveal details. That by the ZESN used national figures; that by the Solidarity Peace Trust attempted, as best it could, to suggest variations within the national figures when they were broken down to provinces, and suggested there could be greater variations when broken down to constituencies and wards. In short, even if the elections had been stolen, they had not been stolen under a uniformly applied plan. The 'plan' produced many local variations. Within those, ZANU-PF might just have got lucky. The MDC was not, by contrast, unlucky. It had not done well in the election campaign, and for its own campaign shortcomings it can only blame itself. Raftopoulos was right to say the electorate had changed. The MDC did not. The Zimbabwe of the 2000s may or may not be better than the Zimbabwe before. Economically it is certainly not better. But it is not the same Zimbabwe that witnessed the birth of the MDC just before the millennium began. Sixteen years is a very long time in politics.

8   One Year after the Elections

How did this 'new' Zimbabwe look to the voters? It was frequently noted that there was little sense of rejoicing immediately after the elections. If Zimbabweans had voted in refreshed numbers for Robert Mugabe and ZANU-PF, many had done so with misgivings, and out of a sense that there was no alternative, rather than with unalloyed enthusiasm. As life settled back down to a pre-GNU normal with Mugabe and ZANU-PF back in charge, and as the MDC noisily imploded, Zimbabweans had time to reflect on their new political settlement.

This chapter returns to the perspective of Zimbabwean voters, and examines what they made of their situation, and their position in the region and wider world, one year after the 2013 election. It begins at a rural secondary school in Mashonaland Central – a ZANU-PF stronghold. This school sits in the middle of a plateau of treeless scrubland, a brave collection of ten concrete block classrooms and nine teachers' houses. All around it are scattered villages, but they are hidden in the dips and folds of the valley as it works its way towards surrounding mountains. Each morning at 8 a.m., children emerge from every direction, following well-trodden paths, collecting in front of the school assembly area to raise the flag and sing the national anthem. During the day they are hidden again, inside the dark classrooms, from which emerge the sounds of teachers explaining, chalk scratching and children murmuring.

But it is the evenings when the place really wakes up, the landscape turned golden by the lowering sun. Then, women and children from all around trek to the pump below the school to draw water. Children linger on the sports fields beside the school to watch football matches and netball training. Teachers and their families sit outside their houses relaxing and tending fires in small thatched kitchens where their supper cooks. And all around there is a hum of a thousand voices laughing and chatting across the valley, lilting back from the hills that surround it.

This secondary school in rural Mashonaland is like hundreds of others. It was built in the early 1980s so that all children could reap the benefits of independence. In those early years, the six existing classrooms were too small to contain the children – and adults – who seized the chance of developing themselves and their new country through education. Pupils squashed themselves into the classrooms, two to a chair, many on the floor; classes were often held under a tree. Across Zimbabwe, hundreds of unqualified teachers – who possessed no more than 'O' levels – were drafted in to cope with the huge demand. This school – like many others – expanded. Expatriate teachers came, then a new generation of qualified teachers. More classrooms were built, a science lab, an administration block, more teachers' houses. Parents fired bricks down by the river and the children carried them four by four on their way to school each day.

In the late 1990s the school was electrified. The teachers got rid of their paraffin lamps and cookers, returning from Harare with electric stoves and television sets on top of the bus. Electricity was put into the classrooms so that the children could come and study at night.

Electricity is a powerful symbol of development, and education for Zimbabweans is seen as the driver of development. Together, electricity and education were going to propel the country towards modernity. But electrification did not come to much of rural Zimbabwe. The arrival of the first generation of newly qualified teachers in 1991–2 coincided with a severe drought and a World Bank structural adjustment programme. The first undermined the country's agricultural exports and the second crushed existing manufacturing, eroding local production. School graduates found there were few job prospects in the formal sector for them. In 2000 many white farms were confiscated, leaving thousands of farm workers without a livelihood. Agricultural exports took a sharp downturn. By 2008 hyper-inflation had caused near starvation across the country.

Now, in 2014, with the economy precarious but stable, a third generation of Zimbabweans are attending the school, sent by parents and grandparents who were the first rural inhabitants to get a secondary school education. But – like the development that it was supposed to bring – many now believe that education has become an empty gesture.

The children seem to keep coming out of habit, and because it gets them out of the boredom and hard work of household chores. Few parents pay fees anymore. When the teachers organised a parents' evening a few months ago, not a single parent came. The electricity wires in the classrooms were stolen within days; the head teacher has lost count of the number of times she has had to replace the perimeter fence.

The teachers say the parents are ignorant and narrow-minded: they can afford fees but choose not to bother; they show no interest in the idea of their children progressing, preferring to keep them at home to help with the cattle and maize. They steal from the school at any opportunity. The parents say the teachers are self-interested and lazy: they don't always turn up to teach and yet they enjoy a good salary and free accommodation. All agree that the benefits of education are at best slim: with the economy so weak and the formal sector all but wiped out, there are few job opportunities for a new generation of literate Zimbabweans. Teaching, which is now relatively badly paid, is one of the few options for those with qualifications, but it feels more and more like a pointless endeavour. The school continues in form but none of its stakeholders believe in its original purpose very much, taking from it whatever material benefits on offer.

Exactly one year after the 2013 elections, this very downbeat outlook fitted in with the wider mood in Zimbabwe. The elections had brought home the realisation that there was going to be no great solution to Zimbabwe's problems. This was partly captured in the collapse of the MDC. Having failed in such spectacular fashion, the party was 'tearing itself to pieces', it had 'pressed the delete button'.[1] Even amongst hardcore MDC supporters there was the strong impression that the party could not recover – they had begun to think about the possibility of a new opposition. ZANU-PF, meanwhile, seemed to have retreated from the electorate after its reconnection in 2013. Few expressed knowledge or even interest in the question of Mugabe's successor, other than the fear that 'when he goes, there will be a war'.

As we described in earlier chapters, Mugabe's rhetoric on race, land and liberation tapped effectively into widely held grievances. Support for ZANU-PF may be expedient for many, but it is also ideologically resonant.

But how deeply does it reach, and how much grip can it command as people continue to feel insecure? There are layers of discourse about politics in Mashonaland. On the top level there is the 'Zimbabwe is sparkling' line, told with defiance to a visitor by those who loyally stick to the ruling party line. Mashonaland remains a Mugabe heartland. Here there has been a substantial amount of resettlement and many formerly landless peasants now farm their own plots. This sits on top of historic ties between the inhabitants of the area that was important in the war of independence. Mugabe's rhetoric on liberation, land and race has deep roots here. Gallagher, travelling on a combi bus up to Guruve, was amused when the bus driver, who had been making friendly, romantic overtures the moment before, was unexpectedly stopped short by his phone's ringtone – a clip of one of Mugabe's speeches. 'Shame, shame, shame to the United States of America. Shame, shame, shame to Britain and its allies . . .'[2] Installing such a ringtone was a usefully public demonstration of party loyalty.

---

[1] Comments made by MDC activists in Harare, 30 July 2014 (JG).

[2] This is an extract from Mugabe's speech to the UN General Assembly in 2013. In it, he made a strong attack on the sanctions imposed on Zimbabwe: 'Our small and peaceful country is threatened daily by covetous and bigoted big powers whose hunger for domination and control of other nations and their resources knows no bounds. Shame, shame, shame to the United States of America. Shame, shame, shame to Britain and its allies. Zimbabwe is for Zimbabweans, so are its resources.

One level down are stories about the terrible period in 2008 – where people lived on soya and got so thin they 'could wrap their belts three times around their waists', where no one had soap, and where a journey to collect a salary in Harare would leave you stranded as your pay wouldn't buy you the fare home. Yet these experiences are often detached from politics, appearing immanent, or caused by malevolent forces ranged against the government: the war veterans, sanctions or the international financial system, for example. Mugabe is often a paternal figure in this story, bravely attempting to reign in hardliners or defending Zimbabweans' use of the US dollar. In this version of Zimbabwe's story, the election was calm and peaceful, nothing particularly interesting, the outcome unsurprising.

But deeper still is a strongly cynical streak, a product of years of hardship. In Mashonaland, there was little opportunity for a turn towards the opposition; it was too heavily repressed. MDC supporters kept quiet; people either had to express support for ZANU-PF or disconnect from politics completely. As a result, there was no 'refinding' of the ruling party during the elections, as in other parts of the country. Instead, the 2013 results just revealed the next stage of the ZANU-PF story, one in which rural people know they will have to make their own way as best they can. 'Politics' is something that 'gets in the way', 'spoils good things'.

FROM POLARISATION TO AMBIVALENCE

As already discussed, politics became starkly polarised over the 2000s. Both political parties, and particularly the MDC as it emerged, deliberately highlighted the differences between itself and ZANU-PF as a way to build loyalty and make the idea of shifting allegiance unthinkable to supporters. Polarisation was entrenched through violent confrontation, a mechanism which emphasised the unbridgeable gulf between the

Please remove your illegal and filthy sanctions from my peaceful country. If these sanctions were intended to effect regime change, well, the results of the recent national elections have clearly shown you what they can do' (Mugabe, 2013).

parties, and it was framed in terms of ideological differences. The MDC's self-characterisation as a liberal party that prioritised human rights and democracy, and its emphasis on relationships with Western donors, was explicitly contrasted with ZANU-PF's concern with anti-colonial nationalism, an identification of Zimbabweanness rooted in the land, and theatrical standoffs with the country's white farmers and the West (Ndlovu-Gatsheni 2009; Tendi, 2010).

Both approaches have resonated effectively in Zimbabwe. However, in the very worst times, the MDC was particularly successful in projecting its own version of Zimbabweanness. For many ordinary Zimbabweans, this dichotomy led to a splitting between a bad reality and an idealised good fantasy of statehood (Gallagher, 2013). The bad existing state was represented by ZANU-PF, associated with violence (in episodes such as Gukurahundi in the early 1980s, Murambatsvina in 2005 and election violence in 2005 and 2008), neglect and misman-agement (most acutely experienced in the hyperinflation period in 2007–8), and the erosion of state institutions (seen in the decline in education and healthcare services, the increasing corruption of the police force and partisanship of the legal system). The MDC, on the other hand, could be associated with a good state. For many support-ers this was evidenced in its battles with and persecution at the hands of the government. For others it was seen in its promotion of human rights and democracy – values that sought both to protect the popula-tion from an authoritarian government and embody an ideal rational, developed state. Tsvangirai, who showed great personal bravery and a heroic defiance towards ZANU-PF violence, embodied this ideal too.

However, as we have shown in earlier chapters, polarisation dissipated during the GNU. The MDC became entangled with ZANU-PF, and was increasingly less able to differentiate itself. More-over, many MDC MPs lost touch with constituents and spent their energies on building personal fortunes instead of pursuing national priorities.

The GNU thus demanded the conflation of very different, even contradictory versions of statehood. This phenomenon has been discussed in a number of ways. McGregor, for example, has argued that Zimbabwean civil servants work within both patrimonial and rational-bureaucratic paradigms. She argues that in Zimbabwe, the widening informal patronage networks are not an alternative to the formal state, but are pursued alongside (albeit in tension with) more rational-legal understandings of institutions (2013: 803). In other words the state is seen in various, often-conflicting ways. A similar theme is pursued by Chan and Primorac in their analysis of Zimbabwean politics as 'hybrid', a politics predicated on the bringing together of a 'willingness to cast away the past with a subtle reiteration of a nationalist indebtedness to it'. Here, they argue, the idea of being either/or becomes less plausible: 'it is increasingly difficult to take sides' and Zimbabweans have had to confront a state about which they have mixed feelings (2013: 122).

As we have shown, this ambivalence about politics and the state has come to permeate Zimbabwean society. Many voters rejected the MDC account of statehood, choosing instead to opt for Mugabe's patriotic nationalism and patrimonial politics. But in making the choices they did, many reflected an ambivalent approach to the state more in tune with McGregor's tension between politics as 'eating' and politics as 'law, professional delivery services and the general good' (2013: 803) and Chan and Primorac's 'postmodern politics'.

The picture is complicated by the constraints many voters were under. Apart from the misinformation they experienced, exacerbated by ZANU-PF's control over the state media, many voters were constrained by fear. As we have detailed, memories of the violent reprisals in areas that had voted for the MDC in 2008 guided many voters in rural ZANU-PF strongholds, and amongst the urban poor. Moreover, as Raftopoulos has argued (2013c), the dense and powerful patronage networks that control access to livelihoods in farming, trade and mining tie people into a dependency on the ruling party.

However, alongside these tangible constraints, new choices and opportunities opened up to many voters in 2013. These centred on the kind of state voters felt they wanted, both in terms of the distribution of resources and the form of Zimbabwean identity on offer. Together they established that Zimbabweans could choose to vote for ZANU-PF, holding together in their minds the knowledge of it as constraining, violent and authoritarian; a sense of its close relation to and understanding of them; and the idea of it as best placed to provide for, contain and embody the country. When people voted for ZANU-PF they did so with ambivalent feelings rather than a pure sense of the party either as ideal or inevitable.

This is reflected in the more pragmatic approach to government in Zimbabwe by many civil society organisations. Turning away from the prospects of outside help, from the prospect of the 'good state', they look again at government and reassess what they see. This is a picture of a government divided, with branches working towards different objectives, often against each other. One civil society leader talked about her successful work with the Ministry of Health on AIDS, where officials and ministers seem really keen to make improvements. Others, she told me, are working only towards personal enrichment and to entrench power. But she felt optimistic about the opportunities of working with what she sees as 'progressive' parts of the state.[3]

THE ELECTION AND THE BROADER INTERNATIONAL SCENE

One way to capture the effects on the wider electorate of the politics that culminated in 2013 is to explore the way activists and voters view the various elements of the international community and their role in the elections. This includes the West, particularly the United States, the EU and Britain, the SADC countries, which have been closely involved in Zimbabwe's political arrangements since 2008, and the AU, which sent election observers.

Zimbabwean attitudes towards the West – and particularly Britain – are still deeply imbued with the strong and complex feelings created by the colonial era and its subsequent repudiation by Mugabe.

[3] Interview, Harare, June 2014 (JG).

Many opposition activists and sympathisers have tended to view Western governments as allies, seeing that they criticise Mugabe, and provide moral and financial support to the MDC. This rests on a deep sense of affinity towards Britain which many Zimbabweans feel has shaped the country – people often cite their understanding of and affection for British culture, language, education and manufacturing. For many Zimbabweans Britain represented the lost ideal state during difficult times (Gallagher, 2013), while the surrounding countries are often viewed with suspicion because they support Mugabe.

During the years that we have been researching Zimbabwean attitudes to the wider world, we have frequently been told that Britain or the West should intervene to get rid of Mugabe. But in 2013, only once did such a comment arise, made by a group of women MDC activists in Chitungwiza who were in despair at the size of their electoral defeat:

> We have a problem with politics: how are you going to solve that problem when the one who says I am the owner of Zimbabwe, he won't go, how can we let him go? ... We are looking to other countries to help us. Why can't those Western countries come in? Here in Zimbabwe we are scared of this man. He fights against us if we protest. He sends his people to take us if we are asleep. The SADC supports him so how can we get help? The help that we need from the West – in our elections we need their armies to come and protect us to ensure the election is free and fair. Mugabe brings the observers in his interest, not from the West. We need the army.[4]

This expression of a dichotomy between the West/MDC and SADC/ Mugabe is an example of the sense that Zimbabweans were being asked to choose between a 'modern' or liberal future and a version of the past that is supported by the rest of Africa. It complements discourses about development that are so often linked to education in Zimbabwe. For example, the 'gold standard' of exam qualifications

---

[4] MDC-T activists, Chitungwiza, 3 November 2013 (JG).

was the Cambridge exam board used after Independence. Many people will still refer to their exams as 'Cambridge' qualifications. The exam board has been ditched by the Ministry of Education since the fall-out with Britain, and a new Zimbabwean standard has been adopted instead. Many people are sceptical about whether this constitutes progress. Another example is the stories told about the black farmers who took over plots of formerly white farms but 'didn't know what to do with them'. Many were assumed to have removed their children from school, and to have stopped visiting health clinics, preferring to consult *Nyangas* (traditional healers). There was a strong feeling that Mugabe's rejection of Britain and the white farmers amounted to a rejection of development. 'Britain means development . . . that's where Zimbabweans will look.'[5]

At the same time several of the southern African countries are seen as backward. Zambia, which experienced economic meltdown in the 1970s and 1980s, used to be patronised by Zimbabweans who 'laughed at Zambians coming over the border to buy margarine'.[6] Mozambique and Angola were still engaged in violent civil wars as Zimbabwe enjoyed its first decade of independence, the hallmark of chaotic disorder. South Africa, larger, louder, richer, is viewed by many as unpleasantly violent and vulgar. Zimbabweans tend to compare the surrounding countries unfavourably. Speaking about the fact that so many Zimbabweans had been forced to migrate to South Africa in recent years, one woman said:

> Zimbabweans are not happy to be living in South Africa.
> A Zimbabwean would be more at home living in England than South Africa – they love colour, speed. Zimbabweans like order, they are more on the slow side. We are more laid-back . . . [English is] a language we are comfortable with and the style of life . . . That has been our history, our legacy. That is us.[7]

---

[5] Former factory worker, Chitungwiza, 28 August 2011 (JG).
[6] Trade union activist, Harare, 1 September 2011 (JG).
[7] CSO employee, Harare, 31 August 2011 (JG).

But by the time of the election campaign, this sense of a dichotomy was slipping. The majority of people were becoming more sceptical about British and Western authority, and growing doubts over their intentions and the various interventions they had made. There was criticism from every angle on the sanctions issue, but the key theme to emerge is a suspicion of Western ineptness or bad faith.

Some argued that sanctions had proved counter-productive:

> The sanctions have united people, have created a hero out of someone who had already expired.[8]
>
> Robert Mugabe suffers emotionally with the sanctions, but he also takes advantage of them. He is using those things to his advantage.[9]

Others thought it was a mistake to begin to relax sanctions before the election as this had signalled an easing of pressure on Mugabe:

> They did their job too early. The EU was lifting sanctions too early.[10]

More generally, it appeared that the West had begun to look weak. On the elections, Western governments had been wrong-footed or intimidated by Mugabe:

> The West were quite in between. They had also swallowed this idea that the MDC was going to sweep into power. They had no idea what was going on in the rural areas. They were naïve. They underrated Mugabe. They need to have been more able to see or help in seeing the manipulation ... They should have done more than just wait and see.[11]
>
> My only problem with them is that they cannot articulate the advantageous relationship between them and Zimbabwe. In terms

---

[8] CSO leader, Harare, 4 November 2013 (JG).
[9] MDC-N activist Matabeleland South, 10 November 2013 (JG).
[10] MDC-T activist, Chitungwiza, 3 November 2013 (JG).
[11] MDC-T activist, Chitungwiza, 3 November 2013 (JG).

of relations between Britain and Zimbabwe, there is lots of money flowing, lots of services provided and exchanges happening. The moment Mugabe comes on TV and criticises the West, they all run under the desk.[12]

One man said that people increasingly felt that London – once the destination of choice for large numbers of the Zimbabwean diaspora – had lost much of its lustre:

> People used to admire the UK. That was when most families had relatives there. When they sent home $100 it would make you a billionaire. Now the money they send can't buy you very much.[13]

Whatever the GNU did to perceptions of the MDC, it also shifted Zimbabweans' attitudes towards the wider world, in ways that reflect their own sense of themselves and their government. The idea of the West as a powerful and potentially liberating ally appeared weaker, as its leaders were variously regarded as naïve, uncertain and cowardly. The sanctions policy was viewed as at best muddled. As a source of resources, even through individual remittances, Britain had lost the almost magical quality it once had when a small sum would turn you into a billionaire. And crucially, the West had swallowed the MDC fantasy, and failed to understand the power and attraction of Mugabe. These perceptions of the West's well-meant but inept handling of the election had a sidelining effect – here were players who had become increasingly peripheral to the Zimbabwean story.

This attitude was clearly entrenched a year on from the election, as was made powerfully clear when I (JG) attended a meeting for some 30 civil society representatives organised by the EU in offices in a Harare suburb. Two EU officials at the front clicked through their slides and talked about road maps, five-year plans, pillars, action areas and benchmarks. After a while it became clear that nobody in the audience was listening very carefully: they were all fiddling with their

---

[12] Trade union activist, Harare, 5 November 2013 (JG).

[13] Businessman, Harare, interviewed in Bulawayo, 9 November 2013 (JG).

phones. The EU speakers rushed through their presentation. A couple
of slightly sharp questions followed. The preoccupation was with the
speed with which the EU was attempting to build partnerships with
the government – these civil society representatives who have been at
the rough end of government repression in the past wondered how the
EU knew it was safe to re-engage. Then everyone moved into the
corridor for tea and cakes. Afterwards there was going to be a series
of small breakout sessions to address the specifics of each action area,
but we had to leave. We weren't the only ones though: colleagues
reported later that most people left after tea. One trade union activist
who had attended the meeting said: 'It was just a boring account of the
EU's plans. Who wanted that?'[14]

She argued that there was an increasing perception among CSOs
that Western donors were out of touch. Western donors had called the
election wrong, predicting an MDC victory, and many were now
moving too fast back towards engaging with the ZANU-PF government. This would probably mean a decline in direct support to the
CSOs – something they cannot be expected to support – but they are
also concerned that donors are falling in behind a government that
they do not understand properly. She said: 'The EU don't realise how
split the government itself is. They don't know which bits are worth
engaging with and which aren't.' The EU's motivations are suspect
too, many Zimbabweans believe, as they are now 'rushing to
re-engage for economic benefits'.[15] However, if the EU is off the mark,
Britain is 'off the radar', listening to the wrong people and continually
getting Zimbabwean politics 'all wrong'. Inept, out of touch and
driven by self-interest, foreign donors who once appeared to offer the
prospect of a real alternative and support are now heavily tarnished.

This trade union activist revealed an interesting characteristic
of the rhetoric that is developing on Western donors, and particularly
Britain: it is very similar to the language used to describe the MDC. Of
the MDC she said: 'we refuse to meet and engage with them anymore

[14] Trade union activist, 5 July 2014 (JG).   [15] Ibid.

because they are all over the place'. Of the British she said: 'We haven't met them for several years now. They just don't listen to us ... They do not understand the political situation here at all.'[16]

In contrast, the SADC countries were clearly and heavily implicated in the Zimbabwean elections. Their implication was ambiguous, not to be trusted, even, but it was undeniably important. Many Zimbabweans believed that the SADC countries were either generally in sympathy with ZANU-PF, or bamboozled or intimidated by Mugabe. An exchange between two MDC activists represents the views of many:

> All those liberation movements were subtly working together with ZANU-PF. They were not prepared to let down one of their colleagues ... they helped ZANU to win.
>
> These other presidents were afraid of Robert Mugabe ... Some of those were school kids when Robert Mugabe got into office and he can preach to them hell and brimstone.[17]

Others commented on the self-interest that motivated the SADC leaders' handling of Mugabe, anxious either about their own domestic pressures, working with weak leverage, or out of self-interest:

> Within SADC almost nine countries are having elections this year. They need each other's support.[18]
>
> Everyone thought [South African President Jacob] Zuma was going to not pull punches and he was going to force Mugabe to institute changes. But then, the diamonds. From being on their knees, they could tell South Africa to get lost – they lost power, influence and control.[19]

Alongside the perhaps grudging but deep-rooted respect shown by other regional leaders for Mugabe, and the fear and power he is able to project, Zimbabweans cited the contrasting judgement the SADC

---

[16] Ibid.   [17] MDC-T activists, Chitungwiza, 3 November 2013 (JG).
[18] Trade union activist, Harare, 5 November 2013 (JG).
[19] MDC candidate, Bulawayo, 7 November 2013 (JG).

leaders appear to have made on the opposition. Tsvangirai has been criticised for failing to canvas regional support (Chan, 2005). However this time, many in Zimbabwe believed that the regional leaders were tired of Zimbabwe's problems and actually wanted to oversee the beginning of a new era: they were open to the possibility of Tsvangirai. Some suggested even that they were hoping he would succeed. Yet, it became apparent to many that the MDC leaderships ultimately failed to inspire confidence in the region – much as it had done domestically.

> SADC acts when the opposition acts, not just when it talks ... The South African team had advised the opposition not to participate in the election ... The opposition failed to appeal to citizens and to SADC – they failed to impress everyone that they were a credible government. South Africa was willing to try but the MDC failed.[20]

Fear, comradeship, respect, self-interest and a failure of confidence in the opposition: a ZANU-PF win seemed the safest option for the region.

What is particularly interesting here is the way in which many Zimbabweans attributed their own feelings to the SADC leaders. As described in earlier chapters, Zimbabweans themselves had reassessed what the parties had to offer. ZANU-PF's projection of authority was persuasive, and substantially backed up for many by the unspoken threat of violence. The MDC was weak, indecisive, inconclusive. This can be viewed as a re-evaluation of what Zimbabwe is, what it means to be a Zimbabwean. Less persuasive is an ideal, Western-focused Zimbabwe; in its place sits a Zimbabwe more firmly embedded in the ambiguities of the region. One very dramatic outcome of 2013 was the sense of many Zimbabweans that they are deeply embedded in the complex politics of the region, and that they have perhaps relinquished the idealisation of a Western alternative.[21]

---

[20] CSO leader Bulawayo, 11 November 2013.

[21] For an argument about Zimbabwe's struggles for recognition within Southern Africa, see Gallagher 2015.

Alexander and McGregor point out that Zimbabwe has often offered a 'poor fit' to broader Africanist literature on the state because its particular history entrenched 'ideas of legitimate statehood hinged centrally on law and expertise: [which] offered African avenues for imagining and demanding citizenship' (2013: 751). These ideas have been eroded by economic and political crisis, and by experiences during the GNU period in which ZANU-PF was able to entrench a patronage economy backed up with violence (Raftopoulos, 2013). As a result, citizens' perceptions of the state in Zimbabwe now appear closer to Mbembe's depiction of postcolonial politics across much of the continent. States, he suggests, are viewed both as providers of protection and moral superiority, 'organizer[s] of public happiness' (2001: 31), and wielders of arbitrary violence, woven into the allocation of privileges. His suggestion of this as a complex relationship and a complex basis for the imaginary of the state resonates with current conceptions of state–society relations in Zimbabwe.

What this means in Zimbabwe is a far more ambivalent state–society relationship than has featured before. There is more of an acceptance of a political settlement that is flawed and problematic – even abusive at times – and less of a search for an ideal alternative. The country feels more embedded in its region. Even if some people managed to persuade themselves that 2013 might represent a 'return to the state of independence', they know that the gaps between their aspirations and the abilities and desires of their political leaders are huge. They know too that this is what Zimbabwe is, it is who they are.

9 Succession Battles in the New Zimbabwe

As the electorate came to terms with the new Zimbabwe in the post-election period, the two main parties turned inwards to begin to play out their leadership battles. This chapter gives an account of how these contentious contests were fought between party elites. In particular, it charts the huge split that opened up in ZANU-PF, setting the scene for a changed party of the future. The messiness of the battles within ZANU-PF and the MDC reflect the messiness of the new Zimbabwe. Although, as we will argue, these have largely been fought over personality rather than ideological lines, they reflect the country's continuing struggles over the legacies of liberation, its attempts to create a nationalist modernity, and its complex ambivalence towards it international relationships. Together, these constitute the 'thinkability' that is shaping the new Zimbabwe.

After the elections, intense divisions within ZANU-PF were for a time 'managed', while intense divisions within the MDC quickly prised the party apart. ZANU-PF, once it had fulfilled its 62 per cent ambition, realised that the opposition could pose no threat to it for at least ten years. President Mugabe could say to himself that he had, with the 2013 elections, bequeathed a legacy of continuity to ZANU-PF. This was a continuity only partially eroded by the need for a coalition government from 2008 to 2013; effectively it stretched 38 years from independence in 1980 to 2018, and quite possibly would last 43 years until the elections of 2023.

Mugabe himself, having won the leadership of ZANU-PF in 1975, had already by 2013 led the party for 38 years and the country for 33. He was 89 in 2013 and the rumours, not so much of his illness – these were always lacking in precision – but of his constant rejuvenation in a Singapore clinic were disingenuously denied by his own office and party. He had, according to those sources, a recurring eye problem that required treatment in Singapore. That he would fairly bounce off the plane on his return to Zimbabwe, his vigour contrasting markedly with the tired and stumbling figure that had left it, fuelled speculation on the nature of his treatment. The rumour mill, by 2013, settled on blood-washing – complete replacement of his blood by transfusions replete with steroids, added red corpuscles, iron additives and anti-inflammatories. The rumours might have added moderate chemotherapy if they had been certain of the stories of a chronic but treatable cancer. Rumour settled on cancer of the prostrate.

All this was to the effect that, ten more years or not of ZANU-PF at the helm of the country, it would not be ten more years of Robert Mugabe at the helm of ZANU-PF. He had bequeathed a further decade to the party. It was time now for him to begin to go, and he could go in a blaze of glory, preferably not in a lingering way, yet with no pressing need to rush. Even within ZANU-PF a form of wishfulness in that direction began to be felt.

There were three other key reasons to ponder the inauguration, not just of a succession, but a formal and visible succession process. The formality and visibility of it all would act as a confidence-building measure, both to external and internal interests. In addition, ZANU-PF is a party assiduously anxious to be seen as following its rules – even if it has had to apply new rules *ex post facto*, as it did when it legalised the land seizures that began illegally in 2000.

The first key reason was that some residual European, but also US sanctions, remained in place and there would not be full re-investment in the country until they were lifted. The lifting would be a signal, awaited by many significant investors, that the country was no longer 'black-listed'. Other liquidity flows from, or facilitated by, Western powers had been tied to the hope of helping an opposition party within a shared government. Those would now dry up with the government no longer shared. President Mugabe was the key impediment to the final lifting of sanctions, as the West had long personalised its view of Zimbabwe; future business with the country was on a 'with anyone else but' basis. The second key reason was that ZANU-PF had succeeded because it was a party with strength in-depth. This meant across all sectors and all generations. There was push from below for upwards mobility, both to propel younger people up the hierarchy and to modernise what could sometimes, even within ZANU-PF, seem a rather antique version of a nationalist project.

A third external reason was also compelling. The SADC states, having validated the electoral victory in the hope of regional stability, now wanted that stability vouchsafed into a medium- to longer-term future. A lingering and declining Robert Mugabe could not be in the regional interest. SADC was in a hurry to reinstall Zimbabwe as a fully functioning member, punching its weight alongside the economically burgeoning Angola and Namibia, the economically strong Botswana, the fitful economy of South Africa, and even the fitfully but visibly growing economic capacity of Zambia. In particular, the South Africans needed Western economic investment into Zimbabwe to establish a palatable risk-shared environment for its own business investments. Even the most nationalist securitised oligarch in Zimbabwe would know that his or her best interests lay in a more fully internationalised economy. The problem with the Zimbabwean nationalist project was that Zimbabwe was simply too small to allow that project to be also a fully functioning modern one. Ownership of everything, including ownership of inadequate economic capacity to generate wealth on a continual basis – so that economic benefit could be both accumulated and diffused to attract future votes – could lead to nothing but ownership. The months after the election, and the slowly but surely growing economic malaise that once again began to grip the country, rammed home the message that ownership was not the same thing as economic generation.

The issue of succession raised its head immediately after the election of 2013, with a lengthy delay in announcing Mugabe's cabinet. For weeks after the announcement was finally made, pundits poured over the appointments for clues as to whether Joice Mujuru or Emerson Mnangagwa had emerged stronger. Mujuru, for her part, even before the cabinet announcement, was suggesting in public fora that she would make a fine next President.[1] She even kicked a football for a photo opportunity – notwithstanding the extra girth she had acquired since her liberation fighting days.[2]

The surprise inclusion in the Cabinet was Professor Jonathan Moyo – even though he had been one of the few losers in the parliamentary race, and Mugabe had earlier indicated he would not select such people for ministerial posts. Closely identified with Mnangagwa for some time up till then, he was also renowned as a highly ambitious political tactician. Moyo's appointment was read as evidence of Mnangagwa's muscle, and his insistence that a close ally should be alongside him in the Cabinet. Otherwise, the Cabinet appointments gave rise to exercises in reading tea leaves where all the tea leaves looked alike. There are two key distinguishing characteristics of any ZANU-PF Cabinet – all members believed in a nationalist project where there is ownership of the means of production (this is simultaneously a nationalism, depicted as an African traditionalism when applied to land, and a vestigial Marxism), and all members knew one another and, even if currently feuding, had worked intimately with one another. Distinguishing one person's 'ally' from another person's 'friend' could be unrewarding in a set of stable (they're all in it together) if fluctuating (within a broad band of stability) relationships and alliances. Whether that broad band of stability would remain became a key question.

THE MDC AND ITS FRAGMENTATION

While ZANU-PF could keep its struggles and individual ambitions shielded, the struggles within the MDC erupted into public view after the 2013 elections. Notwithstanding an extensive float of dissatisfactions with the electoral process – seen by the MDC as rigged and by a

---

[1] *Daily News on Sunday*, 18–24 August 2013: 1.   [2] *Daily News*, 19 Augus 2013: 1.

huge number of civil society groups as significantly conditioned on behalf of ZANU-PF – the leadership of Morgan Tsvangirai, his expensive tastes and his sexual proclivities, his lack of clear new policies, and his lacklustre track record of opposition to ZANU-PF policies (he did not defeat a single ZANU-PF policy) brought him into focus as a key impediment to any opposition project going forward.

In the weeks that Mugabe dithered over his Cabinet, the MDC began its fragmentation. Blame for the defeat, and where it should be attributed, began to reopen old wounds – not least between Tsvangirai and his highly successful finance minister, Tendai Biti. Biti had always despaired of Tsvangirai's lack of consistency in policy formulation, and now it was clear he pointed a finger at Tsvangirai for the comprehensive defeat of the MDC in the elections. Even ZANU-PF hardliners would have accepted Biti in Cabinet, but Biti made it clear he would refuse such an offer and that his loyalty lay with the MDC. But what type of MDC, or even which MDC was it to be? If Biti was declaring himself out of any new coalition, the rumour mill at one stage had it that Tsvangirai was tempted to want in. That would certainly have divided a party licking its wounds with great rancour.

Moreover, if ZANU-PF was kept together, in part, by a view of shares in an oligarchic economy, the opposition MDC had been, in part, held together by a view of shares in an external donor support of democracy and democratic actors. Cynics might observe that the electoral loss, and the unlikelihood of power in five years' time, demanded an almost immediate rethinking of foreign donor support for the MDC. There is income to be gained in the manipulation of such funding. It makes financial sense to be an oligarch within a facilitating party; it makes financial sense to be a democrat within an opposition party with strong external links. Greg Mills, as noted earlier, made the point of financial greed within the MDC. This was also obliquely recognised as an issue by Brian Raftopoulos. Observers at the 2013 elections reported to us how MDC parliamentary candidates in Matabeleland had campaign budgets of only a few hundred dollars. This contrasted with lavish personal habits at the higher end of the MDC hierarchy and, once again, the multi-uxoriousness of party leader Tsvangirai, his capacity to settle expensive matrimonial claims and his lifestyle suggested income beyond the Prime Minister's salary. Lifestyle and its financing were, however, only a side issue – although a highly visible one – in the rancour that accompanied the MDC postmortem after the elections. The chief issue of contention was that the election had been lost because poorly fought, and blame, and who should be blamed, became the stuff of party debate and fury.

To an extent, the MDC internal issues mirrored those of 2006, when the original formation split in two, with a departing faction led by Welshman Ncube and, a little later, Arthur Mutambara. That split was established on key differences on how internal party consultation and democracy should be conducted, with accusations that Tsvangirai acted in a constantly pre-emptive manner, working with an unelected 'kitchen cabinet', and was not averse to the use of thuggery to ensure his ends were met. There was actually no key split, in 2006, over policy; nor was there in 2013. Once again, issues to do with democracy and consultation, transparency of party processes and thuggery, and corruption as indicated earlier raised their heads. But the key issue was to do with defeat and the lack of organised leadership for victory. Here, Tsvangirai and Biti went bitterly head to head, each claiming to expel the other from the party, and leaving the party or the resultant parties in tatters. Such external donor support of democratic opposition that remained would now be fragmented. Tsvangirai was bullish that he was the only one who could oppose Mugabe – but he had not successfully done so, and in due course it could not be Mugabe who was to be opposed. Tsvangirai enunciated no policies for the new opposition wilderness years, nor did Biti, and both men spoke of capacity to oppose and eventually, at some date in the future – 2018 being spoken of as a wishful hubris – defeat those who had defeated them. How, with what means and with what policies, was not part of the rancour that infused dispute, and dispute rapidly eclipsed debate.

The two men had not for some time seen eye to eye. ZANU-PF had always thought it could work better with Biti than Tsvangirai; indeed, in the last year of the coalition government established after the 2008 elections, Biti and the ZANU-PF governor of the central bank, Gideon Gono, seemed very much a team with a common purpose in safeguarding the economy against excess. Gono himself had many enemies within ZANU-PF, and a self-exonerating book (written in 2008) did him no favours – especially as he had supervised a quantitative easing that resulted in shattered global records for hyper-inflation. Even so, he and Biti did demonstrate the possibility of common cause across party lines for an identifiable species of the national good – no matter who was to blame for the national ills in the first place. In short, Biti embodied the sense of being able to go beyond rhetoric and blame games.

Tsvangirai remained popular as a public figure. The crowds at his electoral rallies had been genuinely admiring. In the 2013 elections, however, he never attempted to appear presidential – as he had in the 2008 rallies – and was greeted as a combative populist, a man of excesses, still with some political principles, yet no longer as Zimbabwe's answer to the huge national domination – in economic as well as political terms – by ZANU-PF. Biti's stabilisation of the economy had also directly facilitated the pathways to regularised wealth for the oligarchs, and the nation realised it would have to follow those pathways, no matter who was in political power. Economic, political and securitised power all resided at that moment however within a national ZANU-PF hegemony. Against that totality, Tsvangirai offered no effective alternative pathway – and seemed, in his personal habits, to be walking where the leaders of ZANU-PF walked. With that walk came the entrenchments of habits to do with the assumed unity of political and personal fiefdom. The MDC was run as if it were his vehicle as much as a popular vehicle of both opposition and government. Some of this was offensive, none of it cohered, and the personality of Tsvangirai became simultaneously something that excited crowds but did not attract votes. There was a sense of national recognition of what regional leaders had long felt: here is a worthy man who is not a president. For Biti, and his followers within the MDC, it was: here is a man who began worthily, did not become president, has no idea how to become president, and runs the party arbitrarily and in a personalised mode.

THE CABINET

The election was barely over when Vice President Joice Mujuru opened a new phase in Zimbabwean politics by declaring she was ready to serve as a future president, and the effort to create a populist image for her began. No one expected calamity, although everyone expected a competition. It was a calm before the storm.

Having, by both fair means and foul, but 'peacefully and credibly' reduced the opposition to a parliamentary rump, and having left MDC leader Morgan Tsvangirai crying foul in an increasingly isolated political wilderness, ZANU-PF no longer had organised enemies of substance. In a way, Tsvangirai and the MDC had acted as the glue that kept ZANU-PF together. Its different factions were united in defending themselves, their party and their oligarchic interests against sometimes powerful challenges. Now that those challenges were no longer powerful, ZANU-PF began to turn upon itself. It was as if the party of combat and liberation had to have combat.

First, however, there was the post-electoral task of appointing a Cabinet. Speculation dogged the days after victory. At Mugabe's final press conference of the elections, where he charmed an assemblage of hard-bitten foreign correspondents from the Western media, Emerson Mnangagwa was present, seated close to Mugabe, and – out of character – constantly smiling. Speculation immediately took shape as to the Vice Presidential stakes, and whether Mujuru would be retained or whether Mnangagwa would be advanced.

Mugabe delayed six weeks before announcing his Cabinet. The longer he took, the more the rumours swirled of jockeying for position behind closed doors. They were not rumours confined only to the Mujuru/Mnangagwa question, but they did involve Joice

Mujuru – who was reportedly seeking to persuade Mugabe to include, from a position of strength but out of magnanimity and a sense of national unity, Morgan Tsvangirai within the Cabinet – perhaps even as the second Vice President. The advantage to Mugabe was that he would not only have a reduced opposition outside government, but a controllable opposition within. The advantage to Mujuru was that she was prepared to cooperate with Tsvangirai and, together, the two Vice Presidents might be able to outflank Mugabe. Mujuru's supporters also reckoned that a Tsvangirai inclusion in government would soften the blow of a ZANU-PF victory in Western camps, and be a lever towards Western re-investment in Zimbabwe.

The other factor in the mix was of course that it was likely to be Mugabe's last government. The Cabinet was therefore anticipated as some kind of signal of what policy direction Mugabe would adopt for his swan song. No one envisaged the turmoil within ZANU-PF only a year ahead – least of all SADC, which elected Mugabe to be its ceremonial chairman in 2014.

In the end, the Cabinet was not a bombshell of any kind. Mujuru retained the senior Vice Presidency. Mnanagagwa became Minister of Justice. Pundits searched the other portfolios as to who had secured which critical ministries for his or her allies. Mnangagwa was probably pleased that his friends were given Defence and Finance – although we reiterate the huge note of caution that up until then the Zimbabwean political elite was one of first-name terms for everyone. Everyone was a 'friend' or familiar. It was a tight circle. What someone would deliver politically was not seen in two people making merry in a bar together. Worst political enemies could be best drinking partners.

Surprise Cabinet inclusions were, as noted earlier, Jonathan Moyo, Mnangagwa's long-time ally, and Didymus Mutasa, appointed a minister in Mugabe's own Presidential office. Many thought Mutasa had long passed his best – but he would come, in the days ahead, to be seen as deeply allied to Joice Mujuru. Of the crop of bright, young, technocratic, new ZANU-PF MPs who had swept aside the MDC parliamentarians, none broke through to the Cabinet. It was largely an older generation holding ground, and largely an accommodation of rival factions with supporters of both, in one way or another, given strength.

THE PERSONALITIES

In this section, we give the sequence of events that built inexorably towards the humiliation of Joice Mujuru, and the elevation of Emerson Mnangagwa – facilitated by a newly energised Grace Mugabe. The dynamics of the process against Mujuru had perhaps to be unrelenting and vituperative, given the immense respect Mujuru's record commanded. Much of the remainder of 2013 passed with no public enmity from senior party members – although rumours abounded of manoeuvres beneath the surface, and certainly of manoeuvres within the provincial party structures and the Youth League and Women's League. As 2014 dawned, the tone of debate changed dramatically. Rhetoric intensified as the ZANU-PF Party Congress drew closer. The importance of this Congress is also described here.

However, one of the features of the rhetoric deployed in the orchestrated lead-in to the Party Congress was its appropriation of liberation motifs – including motifs firmly identified with Joice Mujuru. On 6 October 2014 Grace Mugabe pointedly said that she had been prepared to spill blood during the seizures of white-owned farms, that she herself had (implicitly heroically) participated in one such seizure, and that she had wanted to indicate by her own example that the third *chimurenga* stage of liberation was not easy.[3]

The point here is that Joice Mujuru's *nom de guerre* during the second *chimurenga* liberation struggle of the 1970s had been Teurai Ropa, meaning 'spill blood'. Here, Grace Mugabe had been somewhat brazen but was also testing hazardous ground – for Joice Mujuru's war record had been exemplary and genuinely heroic. There are two indicative stories, the first being well-known, and concerned her standing

---

[3] www.newsday.co.zw/2014/10/08/will-spill-blood-grace [cited 13 February 2015].

to return fire against a Rhodesian attack helicopter in 1974. The speed and command of terrain of these helicopters was immense, and guerrilla response was to fragment as a unit and run in different directions so that the machine guns mounted in the helicopter could not destroy the entire unit. These helicopters were also armoured, so it would take an extremely lucky shot from an AK47 to harm one. It is fair to say that these aircraft struck dread amongst the guerrillas. Mujuru, when her unit was attacked by a helicopter, did not run, but stood her ground and returned fire with her AK47 – and got extremely lucky, as some of her bullets entered an opening in the casing around the rotor engine – and brought down the helicopter. It was a rare victory, and was celebrated not because she got lucky, but had been brave enough to create her own luck.

The second story concerned the 1977 Rhodesian attack on Chimoio, an interconnected string of rear camps used by Mugabe's guerrillas in Mozambique. It included a refugee camp and a hospital, and Mujuru was there, heavily pregnant and close to delivery. It was a huge blow by the Rhodesians against unprepared defences, and a massacre ensued. But Mujuru led a counter-attack, and story has it that, after the battle had ended and the Rhodesians had withdrawn, she was seen sitting on a rock, her smouldering AK47 at her side, knitting booties for the unborn child. So, to courage and luck was added *sangfroid*.

At least Grace Mugabe never claimed cold-bloodedness of any sort, but the rhetoric was designed to demobilise Mujuru's liberation credentials. Other genuinely heroic veterans of the struggle were also 'demobilised' in this way and, as 2014 passed, removed from the Central Committee. One was Rugare Gumbo, a former Minister of Economic Development and party spokesman. Some think he was behind the Baba Jukwa Facebook character in the 2013 election campaign – both because of his closeness to Joice Mujuru and for his impish sense of humour. He was certainly a much-celebrated veteran in the liberation war and close to Solomon Mujuru, the liberation General who married the young Joice. He claimed to be the one who persuaded Solomon Mujuru to support Mugabe in the first place – thus establishing himself as the effective surviving progenitor of Mugabe's rule.[4]

The political spectacle of bitter rhetoric, political demobilisation and marginalisation was such that ZANU-PF may, from 2015, have had to move on from a purely liberation struggle ethos, grounded in the political and military struggles of the 1970s. The leadership of that generation is either old or dying in any case. Its early political leaders, like Herbert Chitepo, and its military commanders, like Josiah Tongogara and Solomon Mujuru, have all died – all three in mysterious circumstances. Gumbo, in his post-sacking interview, lamented that all three were not alive and leading the country[5] – and this was a double counter-attack on Robert Mugabe, who had depended on all three and was rumoured by some to have been involved in the deaths of them all. Heroes' Acre, the shrine-like cemetery outside metropolitan Harare, is well-populated by the generation of the second *chimurenga*, not all of whom fell in battle.

One of Joice Mujuru's key advantages was that she had been very young as a guerrilla fighter. She was barely 19 when she shot down that helicopter. After independence she was the youngest cabinet minister in Mugabe's new government. At the time of the Congress she was still only 59. Her great rival, Emerson Mnangagwa, was 68 – not yet a gerontocrat, but his longevity as a representative of a liberation generation will be shorter-lived than Mujuru's. His military exploits centred around acts of sabotage. He was captured and escaped execution by being too young for the hangman. Neither Mujuru nor Mnangagwa were senior military leaders or in the guerrilla high command, although Mujuru's late husband was a key commander and Mnangagwa began his rise in Mugabe's party before independence came. After independence, Mnangagwa became

---

[4] www.dailynews.co.zw/articles/2014/11/27/gumbo-pours-his-heart-out [cited 27 November 2014].

[5] Ibid.

immensely wealthy through business ventures, often with white partners, and rose politically and with great strategic foresight. Much of
this foresight centred upon the forging of alliances, particularly within
the defence establishment, and the command of ZANU-PF Party
constitutional procedures and possibilities. We shall return to that,
but it should be said that he is a political survivor, and one of his acts
of survival involved emergence from an early failed effort to position
himself as Mugabe's successor.

This failed effort involved a collaboration in 2004 with Jonathan Moyo, a figure of great capacity in spin-doctoring and political
manoeuvring. A former university professor, he had authored a book
on democracy in Zimbabwe and, from time to time, had tried to
position himself as a power behind the Mugabe throne. Moyo was
also closely tied to the orchestration of events leading to the
Congress and, together with Mnangagwa's constitutional expertise,
those who were against Joice Mujuru were able to outflank and
marginalise her. Moyo was MP for Tsholotsho in the west of
Zimbabwe and the 2004 episode is called the Tsholotsho Plot or
the Tsholotsho Coup. It was aimed at forcing President Mugabe to
confront the possibility of standing down, but also to prevent a
power play within ZANU-PF by Solomon and Joice Mujuru. When
it was discovered, Mnangagwa had to work very hard to rehabilitate
himself with Mugabe. The opposing lines at the 2014 Party Congress
were drawn ten years earlier.

Moyo had himself not fought. The pressure from younger
ZANU-PF politicians to be given a place in future Cabinets will one
day grow irresistible. The idea of a liberation ideology will need to
become a liberation mythology that fewer and fewer people will have
lived through – and, of those who did, many fell from grace and power
at the 2014 Party Congress.

TOWARDS THE CONGRESS

The ZANU-PF Congress is different from the annual Party Conference. Held every five years, the Congress is the Party's only elective

organ and determines Party leadership. However, it is not the Congress as a whole that elects its officers; that is done by the Central Committee. Party membership does have a role to play, via specific organs of the Party – as specified in an often opaque and not always accessible Party constitution – in selecting membership of this Central Committee. Mnangagwa became a master of interpreting the Party constitution, but even he could not prevent a head of steam building in favour of Joice Mujuru within the Party's provincial leaderships, Youth League and Women's League, both with representation within the Central Committee. By mid-2014 it had become imperative for the Mnangagwa camp to seize control of the leadership of both Leagues. Bitter in-fighting ensued. Control of the Women's League was a first great triumph, with the announcement in August 2014 that Grace Mugabe would be its designate-leader – requiring endorsement by the Congress itself – but the designation was enough in itself to give her a platform.

However, the constitutional niceties of the Party electoral process were convoluted. Politburo member Webster Shamu was reported as giving this account of the process, having first meticulously calculated how many posts were owed to each province:

> This makes a total of 284 posts from the provinces, while 16 other posts are filled by the President, two Vice Presidents, chairman, 10 Presidential nominees and two women and youth secretaries to make a total of 300 members to the Central Committee.
>
> Posts in the provinces would also be equitably distributed per administrative district, with remainders being allocated based on performance during last year's elections.
>
> The Electoral College will be composed of all district chairpersons from the main, women and youth leagues, provincial executive committee members, national assembly of the youth and women's league, members of the national consultative assembly and outgoing members of the central committee from that province.

The election process will begin with the selection of five
Central Committee members to meet the women's quota. This
will enable the provincial congress co-ordination committee to
identify administrative districts not represented, if any, so as to
ensure equitable distribution of the remaining central committee
positions.[6]

Convoluted to the point of confusing, the quotas for representation
nevertheless meant youth and women's organs had more power over
other selections/elections than seemed the case at first sight. Despite
the complexity of the process, and Mnangagwa's unrivalled knowledge of the process, it still seemed by mid-2014 that Joice Mujuru's
supporters would win a majority on the Central Committee and its
elective apparatus.

When the attacks on Joice Mujuru began, with Grace Mugabe
slowly but surely growing into the role of attack dog, it seemed that
the aim was to humiliate Mujuru sufficiently to persuade her to
declare she had no interest in remaining Party and national Vice
President, and thus abandon her pole position in the Presidential
succession. But Mujuru's credentials had by this time increased as,
to her war and her governmental records, could now be added an
educational record. It became known that her PhD thesis, labori-
ously written over many years, was successful in passing its exam,
and that she would shortly become Dr Mujuru. A PhD was hastily
invented for Grace Mugabe – without any known previous registration at the national university (which awarded it), or known thesis,
or any prior academic preparation except an on-line award from a
Chinese university in Chinese language. The clumsiness of this
effort to declare Grace as equal to Joice was met with derision in
education circles – but as simply another recognition of her new
seniority by many of the Party faithful. A street was duly named
after 'Dr Grace Mugabe'.

---

[6] http://allafrica.com/stories/201411200213.html [cited, 11 February 2015].

Such clumsiness gave way to a one-dimensional but shrill series of denunciations of Mujuru. President Mugabe himself, ostensibly to preserve Party unity, issued an appeal against 'factionalism'. Grace took up this term and began accusing Mujuru as the chief faction-monger. By October 2014, the Congress only two months away, Grace Mugabe's rhetoric reached its height. She went to Mujuru's own home province, Mashonaland Central, having earlier complained about the laziness of unnamed Vice Presidents. She told a stadium of Party supporters, with Jonathan Moyo seated behind her, that the key faction leader came from their province. 'But soon we are going to baby dump your faction leader, come Congress in December.' She accused the same 'faction leader' of being the corrupt owner of diamond mines. She accused the 'faction leader' of having corrupted youth and provincial chairpersons. 'If the President does not dump you, we are personally going to dump you.' And the supporters of the 'faction leader' were also warned: 'Very soon you are going to be dumped too.' An echo of divine right crept into her speech: 'A true leader like President Mugabe will come from God.'[7]

At this stage, President Mugabe himself had not yet begun to attack Joice Mujuru. Whether Grace was implying his support, or trying to force his hand, is unclear. But it is difficult to imagine that a President as authoritarian as Mugabe could not be, at least in some way, endorsing a wife who seemed to have free rein of her mouth. By this stage, notwithstanding setbacks in the provincial Party elections, and the need to separate the Youth league leadership from its popular consensus – which was for Mujuru – the Mnangagwa/Grace Mugabe camp was in full flow. However, it was mindful that it still did not yet have the numbers. The traditional Chiefs and the war veteran leadership seemed inclined towards Mujuru as well. The leader of the war

---

[7] 'You're gone! Grace Mugabe tells Mujuru', *New Zimbabwe*, 16 October 2014. Mugabe too had hinted at divine provenance during the 2008 elections when, in newspaper advertising, he allowed himself to be compared to Moses and to King David – one who, under God's guidance, had liberated the chosen nation and the other who had become its first king.

veterans, a group that had served President Mugabe so well in the 2000 seizure of white-owned farmlands, had to be put onto the Mnangagwa target list.

At a meeting of the Party Politburo on 13 November 2014 the war veterans leader, Jabulani Sibanda, was expelled from the Party. The Party's own spokesman, Rugare Gumbo, described earlier as a supporter of Mujuru, was suspended. Two senior Youth league officials and four provincial chairmen were also demoted. Whether or not Mnangagwa and Grace Mugabe had popular Party support, they now demonstrated that they commanded the Politburo, the ultimate power at the top of the Party structure. President Mugabe himself chaired this meeting. Although Joice Mujuru had won support from nine out of ten provinces before this point in time, it now became clear that the writing was on the wall for her 'faction'. If Mujuru could not save someone as senior as Gumbo, the message sent out was that she could save no one at all. The message was that her supporters should desert her. Even someone like Didymus Mutasa, appointed against all expectations Minister in the President's office, was said to have deserted Mujuru – although, as events were later to prove, such a rumour was probably a veiled threat to Mutasa that he should move.

Moreover, even though it had been hitherto assumed that Mujuru had secured a majority of the Politburo on her side, this first direct entry of President Mugabe into the issue left no one in the Politburo in a mood to defy him. Rumours were that Mugabe feared a putsch against him at the Party Congress; that Mujuru had become too close to Western embassies; that business leaders supported Mujuru because they wanted Mugabe to go so that re-investment could begin. Even so, Mugabe was at that stage not prepared to move against Mujuru herself. An unidentified spokesman said: 'The President could not fire Mujuru because she was not an appointee. She was elected.' This resonated with the sense that ZANU-PF, no matter how draconian in its decisions, sought some sort of constitutional fig leaf for all its actions. 'And that is why he said those who did not want her should vote her out.' The 'divorce', as Mugabe himself went on to say, had to be procedural.[8] At this stage, the Mnangagwa/Grace Mugabe/ and now Robert Mugabe wing of the Party still wanted to win the votes at Congress, and thought that by a political reign of terror they could secure them.

MUJURU'S DEFEAT AND MNANGAGWA'S RISE

On 16 November, after protracted silence, Joice Mujuru issued a press statement. She described the attacks on her as 'relentless'. They were 'false, unsubstantiated, malicious, defamatory and irresponsible'. These were very strong words, given that the First Lady had made many of these attacks. She gave a reason for her silence: that, 'as Vice President of the Republic of Zimbabwe ... it is my duty to stay above partisan politicking'. She, however, said she was breaking her silence because the accusations against her had now escalated to those of treason, of plotting 'to overthrow the legitimate Zimbabwean Government led by His Excellency, the President and First Secretary of ZANU-PF, and Commander in Chief of the Defence Forces, R.G. Mugabe'. She declared she had been elected to office and, effectively, threw down the gauntlet to President Mugabe. She wasn't going anywhere. She wasn't going to stand down. If Mugabe wanted her out of the picture, he would have to find a way of sacking her. It was a dignified but extremely bold press release.[9]

But it was also a statement that seemed to retain some faith in the ZANU-PF electoral process, and in the provisions, however convoluted, of the ZANU-PF constitution. The Mnangagwa effort had been based on reducing her electoral support within the Party, while seeking to force her to resign in the face of the attacks. Reducing her electoral support meant making examples of hitherto esteemed colleagues thought to be supporting Mujuru – and sacking, suspending or

---

[8] 'Mugabe crushes Mujuru as Gumbo falls', *New Zimbabwe*, 13 November 2014.
[9] 'Vice President Joice Mujuru's statement in full', *New Zimbabwe*, 17 November 2014.

demoting them. But Mujuru was certain that, everything notwithstanding, she still had more electoral support than Mnangagwa. It
was a curious faith in Party democracy, on behalf of a Party that had
not gained an international reputation for safeguarding national
democracy.

On 18 November, Grace Mugabe hinted there would be a
moving away from an electoral process. Citing the President's power
under the ZANU-PF constitution to ensure a certain level of female
representation at high Party level – and appointing women even if a
man had been elected to a post – she effectively said that the President
could appoint whomever he wished, election or no election. This
applied even to the Vice Presidency of the country. 'It's up to him.'[10]
On the evening of 22 November, President Mugabe, at an all-night
meeting of the Party Politburo, had the ZANU-PF constitution
changed. He could now simply declare who were to be his Party
Vice Presidents. They would be his personal appointees. Even the
ZANU-PF spokesperson declared that 'far-reaching amendments'
had been made to the Party constitution.[11] In the Party, Mugabe was
now stronger than ever. On 26 November, it was announced that
Mujuru – her electoral papers apparently out of order – could no longer
stand for re-election to the Party Central Committee. The same fate
befell almost 50 of her remaining supporters. Without being a member
of the Central Committee, election or no, she could not be considered
for the Party Vice-Presidency. She had dared Mugabe to sack her.
Now, she was sacked.

One of the early victims of what was by now a full-blooded
Party-purge, liberation hero Rugare Gumbo, launched a stinging
attack on President Mugabe – and became the first senior person in
the protracted build-up to the Party Congress to name him as the key
figure at fault.

[10] 'Mnangagwa to become Vice-President', The Zimbabwe Independent, 22
November 2014.
[11] www.news24.com/Africa/Zimbabwe/Mugabe-tightens-grip-on-Zanu-PF-to-choose-
successor-20141123 [cited 23 November 2014].

We have a serious leadership crisis and the whole world is aware of that. We have a leadership that is disjointed, a leadership that has no focus on how to resolve major issues. We have a leadership that is power-hungry and will do anything to subvert the will of the people. They want to remain leaders forever at the expense of the suffering majority ... Mugabe has lost direction and he is being used by power-hungry people. He has practically lost control of the party. He should not have allowed the First Lady to attack long-time comrades like that; and that on its own shows he is no longer in control. He has no vision. You cannot bulldoze amendments to the constitution so that it fits into what opportunists want.[12]

Gumbo was wrong to suggest Mugabe had lost control of the Party. He had in fact reasserted it. But he was right in implying that it was no longer the Party of comrades. For Mugabe's part, he seems to have believed the rumours that Joice Mujuru was plotting to overturn him. The Party Congress began in the first week of December. Joice Mujuru chose not to attend. On 4 December, in front of 10,000 delegates, President Mugabe laid into Mujuru: 'Thieves never succeed ... look at all the transgressions. Her corruption is now exposed.' In Shona language, though not in English, he point-blank accused Mujuru of planning his assassination.[13]

But, if there was a rationale behind Mugabe's actions, he expressed that it was a need to safeguard the country from recolonisation. Mujuru was clearly seen as having become too close to the West. However, Mugabe for the first time gave a hint that he recognised his mortality. Speaking of liberation leaders who had died before him, he said to the Congress: 'So we will go also those of us in leadership one day.'[14] Often, at the Congress, he seemed disoriented. More than

---

[12] www.zimbabwesituation.com/news/zimsit_w_gumbo-savages-faltering-Mugabe/ 28 November 2014 [cited 28 November 2014].

[13] www.bbc.co.uk/news/world-africa-30334209, 4 December 2014 [cited 4 December 2014].

[14] www.zimbabwesituation.com/news/zimsit_w_end-of-an-era-looms, 5 December 2014 [cited 5 December 2014].

once, Grace Mugabe finished his sentence for him. He seemed to suggest that Morgan Tsvangirai had, after all, won the 2008 elections, before hurriedly correcting himself. He seemed in command of his Party but not always of himself. Later in December he would go again to Singapore.

On 8 December 2014, Mujuru issued another statement, using the same dignified language as before, but this time protesting her innocence of the accusations made against her, her loyalty to Mugabe, and – pointedly – iterated a policy programme for Zimbabwe. It included food security, health care, education, transport, urban cleanliness, reliable electricity and water – all the things not discussed at the Congress. As with her earlier press statement, she signed it 'Dr Joice Teurai Ropa Mujuru'.[15] If she was loyal to President Mugabe, this was a finger pointing at Grace Mugabe. Mujuru was the real doctor of philosophy, not Grace. Mujuru, as Teurai Ropa, had been the fighter for liberation, not Grace.

On 9 December 2014, President Mugabe formally sacked Mujuru as national Vice President, together with seven other Ministers and one Deputy Minister. She no longer had allies left in Cabinet. One of the sacked Ministers was Didymus Mutasa, up to then responsible for Presidential Affairs. On 10 December, Emerson Mnangagwa was appointed by Mugabe to the post of national senior Vice President. Mugabe emphasised that his new deputy had no other functions but to take orders from him. In response Mnangagwa prostrated himself on the floor before Mugabe. For Didymus Mutasa, it was all too much. The iron apologist for Mugabe's regime for many long years, he now launched a venomous attack on his former leader. He used none of Mujuru's restraint:

> In the build-up to this illegal congress, it became clear that this clique of evil plotters had successfully waylaid Amai Grace Mugabe and Comrade Robert Gabriel Mugabe and started using them as

---

[15] 'New statement by Vice President Mujuru', *New Zimbabwe*, 8 December 2014.

weapons to unleash venomous and uncouth statements against anyone they perceived to be standing for the original Zanu PF values, ideals and ethos. (President Mugabe's) customary clear and unequivocal stance did not come until this undemocratic congress. In disbelief, Zanu PF and the whole nation listened to their leader berating his own protégés not only in the party, but in government and the august House of Parliament. It will go down in the annals of our Zanu PF history that for the first time the elected leader alienated himself from the people by this behavior. Instead of mapping the road for Zimbabwe's economic recovery and major policies uplifting our people, the congress became a farce and degenerated into a praise and worship playhouse. We strongly and regrettably bemoan the fact that this clique has robbed President RG Mugabe of his legacy as a unifier, a rational thinker.[16]

Mutasa promised legal action against the 'illegal' conduct of the Congress. Amazingly, he was not expelled from the Party immediately for such a full-frontal attack on the President. A Party disciplinary committee was to decide his fate, but the delay suggested that Mutasa and Mujuru still commanded much support within a divided Party.

SATURN EATS HIS CHILDREN

What Morgan Tsvangirai's opposition MDC could never do was now being done by ZANU-PF itself: turning a core part of the Party against the President, and identifying the cause of the national economic malaise firmly with the President and those who had beguiled and used him to secure what seemed like the succession. Whether it was the anointing of a chosen successor or not – some still wondered whether Mnangagwa was merely a stalking horse for Grace to establish a Mugabe dynasty – the disruption to Party unity was such that a re-anointment would be far too costly in the short term to manage. Yet the ethos of the Party, its nationalist project, was such that it

---

[16] 'Zanu PF split imminent as Mujuru confronts Mugabe', *News Day*, 13 January 2015.

seemed unlikely Joice Mujuru, Didymus Mutasa, Rugare Gumbo and the other victims of the purge would form a new party. The amazing patience of the liberation struggle might reappear to encourage a long game to be played.

The West, certainly, would have liked a Mujuru succession. Mugabe's fears of a 'recolonisation' would then seem to have some foundation – except that a re-engagement with the West is not a re-enactment of colonisation by the West. Mugabe thinks in historical terms, the terms of his time as a young struggler against white rule. But the world has moved on. An international economic and financial system cannot be avoided. And China is as much its owner as the West. Mujuru's appreciation of the world-as-it-is was greater than Mugabe's. She knew the nationalist project needed updating and nuancing if it was to be robust enough to fight some corner for Zimbabwe in the brave new world. In that sense, ZANU-PF missed an opportunity to be part of the world. Emerson Mnangagwa could well re-invent himself to become a darling of the West, of China and of the international system. He had, after all, the arch spin-doctor, Jonathan Moyo, on his side. But he would need to have all of the Party and then the nation on his side too. And, with the new appointment to the Finance portfolio, Patrick Chinamasa, hard at work courting Western investors, and promising them in private conversations all manner of exemptions from the indigenisation programme promulgated by ZANU-PF as a key 2013 election plank, the future of the country was bound to be volatile and unpredictable. The election of 2013 brought victory to ZANU-PF, and changed ZANU-PF, just as it changed Zimbabwe itself. The volatile process of change continued for some time to come.

Postscript
On Reality and Rumours

As we argued in the introduction to this book, one of the hazards of working particularly in Zimbabwe is the rumour mill that envelops all political society. In some ways, the rumour mill determines political society as its members react to rumours that someone or another is plotting against them, or, if someone is not plotting against them whether or not they have diminished in importance to feature no longer in a rival's calculations. In this postscript, we attempt to separate those things which have attached evidence from those which are rumours – that may nonetheless either be true or, by force of people's reactions to them, become true. In this chapter they are listed as rumours pure and simple – but they do indicate, deep in 2015 and into 2016, the surreal nature of Zimbabwean politics and, if great care is not taken, of political analysis. Dominating everything is talk of whether or not, when, if ever, the 'old man' might die. It is a political form of 'waiting for Godot', and the talk about it moves sometimes from the surreal to the absurd. But, while it dominates all talk of possible futures, the present remains flat, with few apparent directions forwards or, to use the elevator metaphor, upwards.

And, with the 2016 acute shortage of dollars, panic began to set into the Zimbabwean body politic. If the elevator could not move upwards, it seemed it could again move downwards towards a deep basement.

WHAT IS REAL OR AT LEAST REALISTIC

1 The National Debt

In August 2015 the national debt to multilateral lending institutions was huge. Even in 2013, in the final months of the coalition government, the entire debt – multilateral and bilateral – was $US10.7 billion. This was about 107 per cent of GNP.[1] Granted that productivity was very low, it meant a debt that was unsustainable. At that time, Tendai Biti was still Minister of Finance and arranged a renewal of engagement with the IMF. In August 2015 an IMF team was about to come to Harare for a review of its provisions for (quite modest) assistance. That assistance was to ensure the absence of fiscal collapse, some debt management, some possible debt restructuring – but no debt relief. Zimbabwe owed the IMF itself $US124 million. It owed the African Development Bank $US726 million and was in arrears of $US528. It owed the World Bank $US1.3 billion and was $US926 million in arrears.[2] The country had no capacity to meet its arrears and its only really viable prospect would be a loan from the IMF to repay some part of its arrears to the World Bank – but this would simply be a smoke-and-mirrors gesture which would not diminish the actual overall debt.

The IMF re-engagement engineered by Biti was by means of a Staff Monitored Programme. At the end of August 2015 the visiting IMF Staff Monitored Programme (SMP) team would conduct its second review, the previous review having taken place in April 2015. This meant frequent review over short periods. The SMPs are moreover essentially informal IMF mechanisms, that is they are not formal instruments over a protracted period of time – they are able to be ended swiftly and at short notice. One of the measures agreed under previous review was that Zimbabwe would make regular, albeit modest, loan repayments. So, to the IMF, the African Development Bank, and to the World Bank, Zimbabwe had begun repaying $US4 million per quarter each. Given the overall debts and arrears, these were drops in the bucket – and similar repayments were due to commence to the European Bank[3] – but the idea was two-fold, to suggest good faith and to instigate a process which might involve

---

[1] not dated, but circa. June 2013.   [2] 28 January 2015.
[3] *The Herald*, 18 August 2015: B1.

higher repayments at a later unspecified date. It hardly restored confidence in Zimbabwe, but it was a small step towards regularity in the parlous country's fiscal relationships and obligations.

Even so, the small step was expensive, and Zimbabwe soon found that even modest repayments soaked up sufficient dollars for there to be increasingly insufficient dollars for local circulation.

2 Wishing to Have It Both Ways

But if it was a programme of small steps towards discipline, that discipline was not apparent in being able to sustain cost reductions in an over-manned economy. The country was unable to produce more because of a lack of foreign investment; it was beginning to repay small amounts of debt, but it was having trouble spending less. After a July 2015 ruling by the Supreme Court, some 20,000 people were served dismissal notices, and more were slated to follow. The ruling allowed dismissal without significant compensation upon three months' notice. This opened a floodgate as the expense of previous compensation levels had deterred companies from reducing their workforces. The parastatal Zimbabwe Broadcasting Corporation fired 300 employees, including many senior executives. The local government minister intervened in late August to prevent Harare City Council from dismissing 3,000 employees.[4] And, in the same month, Parliament – now comprehensively dominated by ZANU-PF – passed the Labour Amendment Bill, restoring certain levels of compensation.[5] Whether it would benefit those fired before the bill's passage was unclear – but the legislators seemed undeterred by the possibility of retrospective law and the precedent and problems it might set, whereby law-abiding activity in any present time could be declared illegal at any future time.[6] Behaving legally would then require a crystal ball.

[4] *The Herald*, 20 August 2015: 1.   [5] *The Herald*, 19 August 20115: 1.
[6] *The Sunday Mail* (Harare), 16 August 2015: 1.

The farrago of public sector institutions seeking to become cost-effective, but prevented from doing so at ministerial and Parliamentary levels, echoed a similar about-turn earlier in the year when the finance minister, with clear Cabinet approval, announced a suspension of certain employee benefits, only to have it overruled by President Mugabe shortly after – notwithstanding that the President chaired the Cabinet.[7] The ZANU-PF Government is torn between wishing to re-enter international life as a prudent, well-managed concern that is overcoming its problems, and a dread of losing public popularity – even though it has no effective political opposition.

But, even if the ZANU-PF Government kept the entire public sector in employment, it would have to find the dollars to pay the salaries. Once fail that, and public popularity – or toleration – would plummet. Public service employees were the only breadwinners in an increasing number of extended families, as the formal sector continued to shrink, and no other income was available.

3   The Politics of the Elevator

While the elevator maintained its inexorable descent, politics allowed one anomaly within a ZANU-PF triumph that had carried over from the 2013 elections. This concerned some ameliorations to the indigenisation laws and allowed discretionary sectoral variations.[8] The IMF in its reviews considered this progress as a step towards reassuring an international investment community. Still, it was not enough for the volume and scale of investment the economy required – which were figures in the billions and not millions. To compromise the indigenisation laws sufficiently for such investment would have been a very clear row-back from the centerpiece of the ZANU-PF 2013 electoral platform. However, to the extent that even minor amendments were conceded, this was a triumph for the country's need for

---

[7] www.newsday.co.zw/2015/04/22/mugabe-bonus-decision-dashes-recovery-prospects/.

[8] www.theindependent.co.zw/2015/06/19/govt-in-indigenisation-climbdown.

international outreach as opposed to the government's quest for domestic popularity via a nationalist and nationalisation agenda.

In other developments, an attempt by Didymus Mutasa and Ruagare Gumbo to legally challenge their expulsions from ZANU-PF failed: the ZANU-PF Congress decisions stood. The announcement of a new ZANU-PF party did lead to Joice Mujuru launching it with herself as head. This was after a sustained and studied silence on her part. But the launch was a huge failure. Among other things it meant Tsvangirai's MDC had no opposition allies that could promise any significant numbers of deserters from ZANU-PF. Tsvangirai in the meantime continued to repeat old mistakes, imposing unpopular candidates upon local polities.[9]

More devastatingly, the by-elections called as a result of the Tendai Biti faction having to leave Parliament were boycotted by MDC-Tsvangirai, and all the vacant seats were won by ZANU-PF, swelling its Parliamentary strength and further reducing that under Tsvangirai's command.[10] With a huge majority in Parliament, with no declared prospective Presidential rival other than a diminished Tsvangirai, ZANU-PF should have felt secure and assumed a smooth ride into the 2018 elections. Already, in the second half of 2015, the mood was looking forward, hopefully/fancifully/fatalistically towards 2018. But 2016 saw calamities begin to sink in, even without an organised and strong formal opposition.

WHAT WAS RUMOUR?

Why did Tsvangirai boycott the by-elections? Did he think he had insufficient electoral strength? Rumour had it that he had been advised by Botswana's President Khama, an ally in the vexed aftermath of the 2008 elections, at a regional summit in Maputo, Mozambique, that the vote would be rigged. But why would ZANU-PF rig the

[9] www.thestandard.co.zw/2015/08/17/tsvangirai-endorses-banda.
[10] www.voazimbabwe.com/content/zimbabwe-election-results-2015-harare-bulawayo/2816924.html, 11 June 2015.

vote? It already had a two-thirds majority in Parliament, and increasing it would have availed it no further Parliamentary advantage whatsoever. Perhaps Tsvangirai was simply tired by this stage, but his very small share of the Parliamentary seats would not help him in the campaigns of 2018 – especially if he would be up against one or the other of the Mugabes.

The second of the great rumours swirling around Harare as the end of 2015 was that Grace Mugabe had no significant senior support within ZANU-PF. She had been used as an attack-dog against Joice Mujuru, and although she had clearly warmed to the role of demagogue, her lack of liberation history, ministerial experience (or capacity, her detractors said) and independent power base acted against her. Moreover, her new-found taste for demagoguery had led her to preemptory criticisms of her ZANU-PF colleagues and she had developed, without at all needing to, enemies within. She was also rumoured to be ill, possibly with cancer. If death didn't take her before her husband, the rumours said, she would be prevented from making a run in 2018. But, as events unfolded, it increasingly seemed that this was wishful thinking on the part of those who came from the party's past.

And it was said that much depended on who controlled an elite intelligence/dirty-tricks/assassination unit within the Presidential State House. An intelligence 'Praetorian Guard', it was supposedly independent of the Central Intelligence Organisation and the military, and its existence had not been mooted before 2015. Now it was said to be the unit that had engineered the 2011 death/assassination/clinical-and-professional-execution of Solomon Mujuru. Some even said it was the unit that engineered electoral rigging – although a nationwide rigging capacity could not be the work of one small unit. But what such rumours suggested was that Zimbabwean politics now seemed to enter new depths even further away from transparency than before. Plots and counter-plots brewed and hatched and the rumour mill became at times unbelievable because everything began to seem fanciful and fantastic. Rome was burning and everyone was buying new fiddles.

THE OUTLOOK TOWARDS 2018

The problems with the Zimbabwean economy were both indebtedness and a lack of productivity. A small GNP meant debt in excess of GNP; but, even if GNP improved dramatically, few countries could sustain debt at, say, 80 per cent of GNP. For Zimbabwe, this would be a marked improvement from 107 per cent. In early 2015, growth was forecast as 3.2 per cent for the coming year. By August, this had been revised down to 2.8 per cent. By the time of President Mugabe's speech to Parliament in the third week of August – a speech in which his economic forecasts were roundly heckled by the surviving MDC Parliamentarians – it was 1.5 per cent. This was due, Mugabe said, to falling agricultural production.[11] Here, the lack of planning in the farm seizures and nationalisations from 2000 onwards were continuing their long homewards roost. Nothing in the seizures noted that the productivity of the land was agri-industrially-based, and that this could not be maintained by amateurs – who may have loved the land to be sure, but did not have technical knowledge of dams, fertilisers, pesticides and markets. The fall in agricultural productivity in 2015 meant not only diminished economic growth, and therefore no real change in the productivity to debt ratio, it meant malnutrition and hunger would once again stalk the countryside – and, once again, Western states castigated regularly by President Mugabe, together with the UN, would uncomplainingly provide food relief.

Yet despite the continuing economic malaise and ZANU-PF's political in-fighting, it is difficult to see how the MDC can regroup to present a viable challenge in 2018. The British government no longer provides financial support, and the SADC countries appear to have lost whatever interest they once had in Tsvangirai's party. As we have argued in this book, the MDC lost the 2013 elections as much as ZANU-PF won them.

[11] *Guardian* (London), 26 August 2015.

Morgan Tsvangirai's decision not to contest the by-elections caused by the Biti faction's departure from Parliament mystified observers. He continues to live in the specially constructed (former) Prime Minister's mansion in a 'grace-and-favour' arrangement. He seems not to learn from past mistakes, and seems to have no strategy towards 2018 – except that, once again, as he expected in 2013, 'history' will plainly choose him. Except that, with the announcement in 2016 that he was suffering from cancer of the colon, illness or death might prevent a 2018 run.

There are as yet no viable alternatives. The Biti faction – MDC Renewal – has no electoral machinery, no regional power base and no seats in Parliament. The Mutasa ZANU-People First, increasingly called just People First, has established no base, no organisation and no public presence. The very small grouping around former ZANU-PF technocratic minister, Simba Makoni, remains just that – a very small grouping. Welshman Ncube and Dumiso Dubengwa lost their credibilities as electoral forces in 2013.

On his August 2013 visit, as he entered Zimbabwe, Chan was questioned by CIO operatives: 'What do you think of the prospect of an opposition grand coalition?' What grand coalition? What prospect? These were the only replies possible in the current state of opposition disarray, and they remained the only ones into 2016.

AN ANTIQUARIAN'S LEGACY

2015 was a strange year for the international image of President Robert Mugabe. It began with his stumble from the bottom step of a podium from which he had been making a speech on 4 February. Despite frantic efforts to cover up the fact he had fallen (and thus seemed frail), photographs of the fall went viral; the more the Zimbabwean authorities tried to suppress the image, the more it reappeared in ever more inventive photoshopped guises. The stumbling Mugabe looked perfect riding a surfboard, playing football, chasing women on a beach. The ridicule became almost affectionate. The latter part of the year saw an amazing international solidarity dig in behind Zimbabwe – for the sake of an unjustly assassinated lion called Cecil, shot by a US dentist on 1 July. Even Mugabe realised he had better milk the moment – although he took more than a month to do so – and spoke of the nation's pride in a big cat named after his country's coloniser.[12] But, if it had been a year of pictures of the fall, and pictures of a lion, what about deeper issues to do with what Mugabe leaves behind him? What about the tumultuous year that followed, and the realignment of forces and advent of new forces in 2016?

It is hardly a desirable or comfortable legacy that Mugabe bequeaths. The state is not so much dysfunctional as an assortment of clans and factions that seek to command it for individualised benefit – all with a nostalgia for a once almost modern public sphere that, all the same, could not pull itself away from an ideologised love of antique symbols and opposition to antique enemies; and, above all, a love for the short-term, politicised manipulation of those symbols to no obvious national benefit. The Zimbabwe that stumbles into a post-Mugabe future will be one far behind the practices and obligations of modernity, while pointing to the phantom outlines of what could and perhaps should have been.

And what could be may finally have nothing to do with either ZANU-PF or any opposition party bringing it about. In the second half of 2016, spontaneous urban civil unrest sprang up as unemployment and increasingly late payment of public salaries engendered huge dissatisfaction. A parallel system of bond notes was introduced alongside the ever-scarcer US dollars. Purportedly with the same value as the dollar, and supposedly underpinned by the dollar, these were evidence only that there were not enough dollars and that, once again, a form of printing money had been engineered.

The new protesters were at pains to be seen as patriots. They wrapped themselves in Zimbabwean flags. They protested in non-violent but persistent forms. But they had no programme. They had

[12] www.bbc.co.uk/news/world-africa-33854374 10 August 2015.

no rural support. Nevertheless, in July 2016 they won the support of the war veterans who, to everyone's surprise, declared no confidence in Robert Mugabe. The message seemed also one of no confidence in Grace Mugabe who, by then, had become a fully revived national figure, leading the so-called Group of 40 (G40), which claimed to represent a new generation who had not fought in the liberation war because its members (like Grace) had been too young. But this meant, if they were successful in the power struggle against Emerson Mnangagwa – and Mnangagwa was certainly a besieged figure as 2016 progressed – ZANU-PF would indeed no longer be the party of liberation, except in its history and its mythology. But the G40 also has no programme. And, despite the astonishing return to health and political clout of Grace Mugabe – a feat of no mean accomplishment as Zimbabwean politics became more treacherous and unforgiving – she and the G40 would still need the endorsement of Robert Mugabe, who has less and less to offer the electorate.

We conclude this book therefore with the irony that the 2013 elections were won by Robert Mugabe and ZANU-PF, but they were also elections that led to everything he and his party once stood for facing a total eclipse by the time of the next elections in 2018.

Bibliography

African Union Commission 2013 *Report of African Union Election Observation Mission to the 31 July 2013 Harmonised Elections in the Republic of Zimbabwe*. Addis Ababa: African Union Commission

Alexander, Jocelyn and JoAnn McGregor 2013 'Introduction: politics, patronage and violence in Zimbabwe', *Journal of Southern African Studies* 39(4): 749–63

Alexander, Jocelyn and Kudakwashe Chitofiri 2013 'The Consequences of Violent Politics in Norton, Zimbabwe', in Chan, Stephen and Ranka Primorac, eds.: 73–86

Badza, Simon 2008 'Zimbabwe's 2008 elections and their implications for Africa', *African Security Review* 17(4): 2–16

BBC 2013a 'Zimbabwe's Tsvangirai dismisses election as "huge farce"', BBC News, 1 August 2013: www.bbc.co.uk/news/world-africa-23530796 [cited 26 July 2015]

BBC 2013b 'Zimbabwe election "free and fair", say AU observers', BBC News, 2 August 2013: www.bbc.co.uk/news/world-africa-23550191 [cited 26 July 2015]

BBC 2013c 'Zimbabwe poll "free and peaceful" say Obasanjo and SADC', BBC News, 2 August 2013: www.bbc.co.uk/news/world-africa-23546050 [cited 26 July 2015]

Berting, Pelle 2010 *Divides and Rules: A Dilemma Approach to the Dynamics of Democratisation: The 2005 Parliamentary Elections in Zimbabwe*. Saarbrücken: LAP Lambert

Booysen, Susan 2012 *Change and 'New' Politics in Zimbabwe - Interim Report of a Nationwide Survey of Public Opinion in Zimbabwe: June-July 2012*. Washington DC: Freedom House

Booysen, Susan 2014 'The decline of Zimbabwe's Movement for Democratic Change-Tsvangirai: public opinion polls posting the writing on the wall', *Transformation: Critical Perspectives on Southern Africa* 84: 53–80

Bracking, Sarah 2005 'Development denied: autocratic militarism in post-election Zimbabwe', *ROAPE*, DOI: 10.1080/03056240500329361

Bratton, Michael 2014 *Power Politics in Zimbabwe*. Boulder: Lynne Rienner

Chan, Stephen 2005 *Citizen of Africa: conversations with Morgan Tsvangirai*. Harare: Weaver Press

Chan, Stephen 2007 'Breakthrough in Harare', *Prospect* November

Chan, Stephen 2008 'Taking on the Lion King', *New Statesman* 11 February

Chan, Stephen 2011 *Southern Africa: Old Treacheries and New Deceits*. London and New Haven: Yale University Press

Chan, Stephen and Ranka Primorac, eds. 2013. *Zimbabwe since the Unity Government*. London: Routledge

Chigudu, Daniel 2012 *Perceptions of a free and fair election in Zimbabwe: perceptions on elections*. Saarbrücken: LAP Lambert

Chitiyo, Knox 2009 *The Case for Security Sector Reform in Zimbabwe*, www.rusi .org/downloads/assets/Zimbabwe_SSR_Report.pdf [cited 26 June 2015]

Dewa, Didmus and Tafadzwanashe Muchemwa 2014 'The voter education "ghost" in Zimbabwean harmonised elections of 2008 and 2013: what can be done? Case of Midlands, Gweru District', *International Journal of Research in Humanities and Social Studies* 1(1): 44–55

Dube, Brian and Peter Makaye 2013: 'How ZANU-PF "won" the 2013 harmonized elections in Zimbabwe', *International Journal of Humanities and Social Science Invention* 2(10): 33–9

Gallagher, Julia 2013 'Good state/Bad state: loss and longing in postcolonial Zimbabwe', in Ebenezer Obadare, ed. *The Handbook of African Civil Society*. New York: Sage: 61–75

Gallagher, Julia 2015a 'The battle for Zimbabwe, 2013: from polarisation to ambivalence', *Journal of Modern African Studies*, 53(1): 27–49

Gallagher, Julia 2015b 'Creating a State: a Kleinian reading of recognition in Zimbabwe's regional relationships', *European Journal of International Relations*, DOI: 10.1177/1354066115588204: 1–24

Goredema, Dorothy and Pecyslage Chigora 2014 'Political campaigning and harmonized elections in 2013: examining the strategies', *OSSREA Bulletin* XI(1): 30–40

Hudleston, Sarah 2005 *Face of Courage: Morgan Tsvangirai, A Biography*. Cape Town: Double Storey

Hyden, Goran 2006 *African Politics in Comparative Perspective*. New York: Cambridge University Press

International Crisis Group 2013 *Policy Briefing. Zimbabwe's Elections: Mugabe's Last Stand*, Africa Briefing no.95, Johannesburg and Brussels: International Crisis Group. 29 July 2013

Kamete, Amin Y. 2009 'In the service of tyranny: debating the role of planning in Zimbabwe's urban "clean-up" operation', *Urban Studies* 46(4): 897–922

Kibble, Steve 2013 'Zimbabwe between the referendum and the elections', *Strategic Review for Southern Africa* 35(1): 93–117

Kriger, Norma 2005 'ZANU(PF) strategies in general elections, 1980–2000: discourse and coercion', *African Affairs* 104(414): 1–34

Kriger, Norma 2008 'Zimbabwe's Parliamentary election of 2005: the myth of new electoral laws', *Journal of Southern African Studies* 34(2): 359–78

LeBas, Adrienne 2011 *From Protest to Parties: Party-Building and Democratization in Africa*. Oxford: Oxford University Press

LeBas, Adrienne 2014 'The perils of power sharing', *Journal of Democracy* 25(2): 52–66

Mahomva, Richard Runyararo 2013 'Power struggles in Zimbabwe: the legitimisation of Mugabeism and the future of Zimbabwe after the 2013 fate', *Leaders for Africa Network*

Makumbe, John 2006 'Electoral politics in Zimbabwe: authoritarianism versus the people', *Africa Development* XXXI(3): 45–61

Makumbe, John and Daniel Compagnon 2000 *Behind the Smokescreen: The Politics of Zimbabwe's 1995 General Elections*. Harare: University of Zimbabwe Publications

Mamdani, Mahmood 2008 'Lessons from Zimbabwe', *London Review of Books* 30(23): 17–21

Masunungure, Eldred V. ed. 2009 *Defying the Winds of Change: Zimbabwe's 2008 Elections*. Harare: Weaver Press

Masunungure E. V. and J. M. Shumba, eds. 2012 *Zimbabwe: Mired in Transition*. Harare: Weaver Press

Mbembe, Achille 2001 *On the Postcolony*. London: University of California Press

McGregor, JoAnn 2013 'Surveillance and the City: patronage, power-sharing and the politics of urban control in Zimbabwe', *Journal of Southern African Studies* 39(4): 783–805

Mhanda, Wilfred 2011 *From Liberation Movement to Government: Zimbabwe a Case Study*, essay dated 3 October 2012, copy in the possession of the current authors

Mills, Greg 2011 *Politics and Economics in Zimbabwe – War by Other Means? Finding a Way out of the Crisis*. Johannesburg: Brenthurst Foundation

Moore, David 2006 '"When I am a century old": why Robert Mugabe won't go', in Southall, Roger and Henning Melber, eds. *Legacies of Power: Leadership Change and Former Presidents in African Politics*. Cape Town: Human Sciences Research Council: 120–50

Moore, David 2013a 'Waiting for Elections in 2013: 11 Theses (with Appropriate Apologies) on Zimbabwe's Moment of Magical Realism', http://african arguments.org/2013/06/18/11-theses-with-appropriate-apologies-on-zimbabwe per cente2 per cent80 per cent99s-moment-of-magical-realism-waiting-for-elec tions-in-2013 per cente2 per cent80 per cent94by-david-moore/ [cited 26 June 2015]

Moore, David 2013b 'In Zimbabwe: a lutua continua', OpenCanada.org: http://opencanada.org/features/the-think-tank/comments/in-zimbabwe-la-luta-continua/ [cited 26 June 2015]

Moore, David 2014 'Zimbabwe's democracy in the wake of the 2013 election: contemporary and historical perspectives', *Strategic Review for Southern Africa* 36(1): 47–71

Mugabe, Robert Gabriel 2013 'Statement by His Excellency the President of the Republic of Zimbabwe, Comrade Robert Gabriel Mugabe during the general debate of the 68th session of the United Nations Generally Assembly, New York, on September 26, 2013', Bulawayo24.com: www.bulawayo24.com/index-id-opinion-sc-speeches-byo-36616.html [cited 26 June 2015]

Munaki, Brian 2013: 'Why Tsvangirai will lose the July 31 2013': http://papers.ssrn.com/sol3/papers.cfm?abstract_id=2298746 [cited 28 March 2015]

Murithi, Tim and Aquilina Mawadza eds. 2011 *Zimbabwe in Transition: A View from Within.* Aukland Park: Fanele

Ncube, Cornelias 2013 'The 2013 elections in Zimbabwe: end of an era for human rights discourse?', *Africa Spectrum*, 48(3) 99–110

Ndlovu-Gatsheni, Sabelo 2009 'Making sense of Mugabeism in local and global politics: "So Blair, keep your England and let me keep my Zimbabwe"', *Third World Quarterly* 30(6): 1139–58

Ndlovu-Gatsheni, Sabelo 2012 *Elections in Zimbabwe: A Recipe for Tension or a Remedy for Reconciliation?* Wynberg: Institute for Justice and Reconciliation

Neuhaus, Matthew E.K. 2015 '"A Tale of Three Elections": Zimbabwe, Zambia and Malawi: Trends, Challenges and Regional Relations', speech to Chatham House Roundtable, London, 26 March 2015. Text of speech provided by Matthew Neuhaus.

Onslow, Sue 2011 *Zimbabwe and Political Transition*, London: London School of Economics

Potts, Deborah 2006 '"Restoring order"? Operation Murambatsvina and the urban crisis in Zimbabwe', *Journal of Southern African Studies* 32(2): 273–91

Primorac, Ranka and Stephen Chan, eds. 2007. *Zimbabwe in Crisis: The International Responses and the Space of Silence.* London: Routledge

Raftopoulos, Brian 2007 'Reflections on the Opposition in Zimbabwe: The Politics of the Movement for Democratic Change (MDC)', in Primorac, Ranka and Stephen Chan, eds.: 125–52

Raftopoulos, Brian ed. 2013a *The Hard Road to Reform: The Politics of Zimbabwe's Global Political Agreement.* Harare: Weaver Press

Raftopoulos, Brian 2013b *As Zimbabwe's elections on 31 July approach, the Southern African Development Community is under pressure to complete its mandate from 2007*, circular email posting of 29 July 2013

Raftopoulos, Brian 2013c 'The 2013 elections in Zimbabwe: the end of an era', *Journal of Southern African Studies* 39 (4): 971–88

Raftopoulos, Brian 2014 'Zimbabwean Politics in the Post 2013 Elections Period: The Constraints of Victory', Solidarity Peace Trust electronic mailing, 27 June 2014

Ranger, Terence 2004 'Nationalist historiography, patriotic history and the history of the nation: the struggle over the past in Zimbabwe', *Journal of Southern African Studies*, 30(2): 215–34

Rich Dorman, Sara 2005 '"Make sure they count nicely this time": the politics of elections and election observing in Zimbabwe', *Commonwealth and Comparative Politics* 43(2): 155–77

Rich Dorman, Sara 2016 '"We have not made anybody homeless": regulation and control of urban life in Zimbabwe', *Citizenship Studies* 20(1): 84–98

Rupiya, Martin 2007, 'Calling in the generals', in Moyo, Gugulethu and Mark Ashurst, eds. *The Day after Mugabe: Prospects for Change in Zimbabwe*. London: Africa Research Institute: 62–7

SABC 2013 'Obasanjo describes Zimbabwe elections as credible' www.sabc.co.za/news/a/27a53e80408f9de697349738b59b7441/Obasanjo-describes-Zimbabwe-elections-as-credible-20130108, 1 August 2013 [cited 26 July 2015]

Sachikonye, Lloyd 1990 'The 1990 Zimbabwe elections: a post-mortem', *Review of African Political Economy* 17 (48): 92–9

Sachikonye, Lloyd 2004 'Constitutionalism, the electoral system and challenges for governance and stability', *Zimbabwe Journal of African Elections* 3(1): 140–59

Sachikonye, Lloyd 2011 *When a State Turns on Its Citizens: Institutionalized Violence and Political Culture*. Harare: Weaver Press

SADC 2013a *Preliminary Statement by Hon. Bernard Kamillius Membe, Minister of Foreign Affairs and International Cooperation of the United Republic of Tanazania and Head of the SADC Election Observation Mission to the Harmonised Elections of the Republic of Zimbabwe held on 31 July 2013*. Observation Mission to the Republic of Zimbabwe

SADC 2013b Zimbabwe election: SADC observer mission's summary statement, www.newzimbabwe.com/news-12240-SADC+observer+team+summary+statement/news.aspx, 2 September 2013 [cited 26 June 2015]

SAPES 2013 Statement on the Pre-election Conditions for the 2013 Harmonised Elections, from a special meeting of the SAPES Policy Dialogue Forum, 30 July 2013

Schatzberg, Michael 2001 *Political Legitimacy in Middle Africa: Father, Family, Food*. Bloomington: Indiana University Press

Solidarity Peace Trust 2013 *The End of A Road: The 2013 Elections in Zimbabwe*. Johannesburg: Solidarity Peace Trust, October 2013

Southall, Roger 2013 'How and why ZANU-PF won the 2013 Zimbabwe elections', *Strategic Review for Southern Africa* 35(2): 135–51

Sylvester, Christine 1986 'Zimbabwe's 1985 elections: a search for national mythology', *The Journal of Modern African Studies* 24(1): 229–55

Tendi, Blessing-Miles 2010 *Making History in Mugabe's Zimbabwe: Politics, Intellectuals and the Media*. Oxford: Peter Lang

Tendi, Blessing-Miles 2013 'Robert Mugabe's 2013 Presidential Election Campaign', *Journal of Southern African Studies* 39, 4: 963–70

Tendi, Blessing-Miles 2014 'The Origins and Functions of Demonisation Discourses in Britain–Zimbabwe Relations (2000–)', *Journal of Southern African Studies* 40:6, 1251–69

Waldahl, Ragnar 2004 *Politics and Persuasion 2000: Media Coverage of Zimbabwe's 2000 Election*. Harare: Weaver Press

Zamchiya, Phillan 2013 'The MDC-T's (un) seeing eye in Zimbabwe's 2013 harmonised elections: a technical knockout', *Journal of Southern African Studies* 39, 4: 955–62

Zimbabwe Election Support Network 2013 *Report on the 31 July Harmonised Elections*. Harare: ZESN

Zimbabwe Human Rights NGO Forum 2013 2013 Harmonised Elections Preliminary Statement, circular email, 1 August 2013

Index

academic perspective, 18, 92–4, 117–22,
    127–8
African Development Bank, 169–71
African Renaissance, 29
African Union (AU), 3, 10, 46, 104–5, 110,
    114–15, 117
agriculture. *See* farmers
AIDS, 137
Annan, Kofi, 29–30, 34–5, 91–2
anti-colonial rhetoric, 4–5, 29, 88, 165–6, 168
AU. *See* African Union
authority, 11–14, 119, 135–6. *See also* power
    structures

Biti, Tendai, 41–2, 81, 107–8
    economy stabilisation of, 30–1, 92, 152–3
    faction leaving Parliament, 173, 176
    as minister of finance, 8, 30–1, 169–71
    Tsvangirai, M., conflict with, 8, 126–7,
        150–1
    ZANU-PF on, 152
Blair, Tony, 4
Booysen, Susan, 40–1, 44–6, 97–101, 127
Booysen report. *See* Freedom House survey
Britain, 4–5, 121, 137–9, 141
Bulawayo, 16–17, 47–8

cabinet, 29–30, 148–9, 153–5
campaign financing, 60–2, 66–7, 79–80, 150–1
centenarians, 38, 40–1, 44–5
Central Committee. *See* Congress
Central Intelligence Organisation, 49
China, 168
Chinamasa, Patrick, 41–2, 168
Chitepo, Herbert, 156–7
citizens and society. *See* state–society
        relationship; Zimbabweans
civil liberty. *See* human rights and civil
        liberties
Civil Society Organisation (CSO), 47–8, 53–4,
        71, 137, 141–3
civil unrest, 177–8
class, social. *See* middle class; social class

coalition government. *See* Government of
        National Unity
colonialism, 4–5, 88, 168. *See also*
        anti-colonial rhetoric
Congo. *See* Democratic Republic of Congo
Congress, 158–60, 164–7, 173
constitutional reform, 25–6, 33–5, 37,
        164, 171
corruption, 56–7, 63, 99–100, 120–1, 173–4.
        See also rigging
CSO. *See* Civil Society Organisation
currency, 5, 30–1, 92

debt. *See* national debt
Democratic Republic of Congo, 27–8

economy, 128–9. *See also* currency;
        employment; poverty
    Biti stabilisation efforts for, 30–1, 92,
        152–3
    Freedom House voter survey on, 98
    indigenisation policies impact on, 35–6
    international relations and, 31, 148
    legacy of collapsed, 5–6
    Mugabe, R., on, 175
    national debt and, 169–71, 175
    in South Africa, 148
    Tsvangirai, M., impact on, 33
    2008 elections and downfall of, 25
    after 2013 elections, 148, 171–2, 175
    ZANU-PF resource redistribution and,
        76–8
education, 131–2, 138–9
elderly, 38, 40–1, 44–5, 111–12
elections (1980 to 2000), 19
elections (2005), 12–13, 19–21
elections (2008)
    economic crisis and, 25
    electoral changes in, 25–6
    forecasts for, 26–7
    Kariba summit and, 25
    Makoni in, 24
    MDC in and after, 26–7, 29–30, 47

CPSIA information can be obtained
at www.ICGtesting.com
Printed in the USA
LVHW080730220221
679533LV00052B/2450